AFTER THEY ARE YOURS

The Grace and Grit of Adoption

Brian Borgman
Cruciform Press | October 2014

To Alex, our son.
I thank God for the day He brought you
into our lives.
Love, Dad

Alex, Ariel, and I would also like to lovingly
remember our dear friend and ardent supporter:
Diane Gamble
(12/16/52 – 3/17/14)

– Brian Borgman

CruciformPress

"*After They Are Yours* is a compelling story about saying *yes* to God and then watching the Father shape and redeem his sons and daughters through love, grace, and mercy."

Kelly Rosati, Vice President of Community Outreach, Focus on the Family

"The decision to adopt is heroic. The reality is often hard. This book does not sugar coat the sacrifice that comes standard with adoption. It will help those considering adoption to count the cost. And it will provide encouragement and help for parents who have already welcomed a child into their forever family."

Bob Lepine, Co-Host, *FamilyLife Today*

"It's all here — joy, hurt, and longing. And this is precisely what we most need: truth-telling that plunges beyond cliché and façade to speak of both the beauty and the brokenness that so often come woven together in adoption, all of it wrapped round by God's limitless grace."

Jedd Medefind, President, Christian Alliance for Orphans and author of *Becoming Home*

"It's one thing to tell the truth about being an adoptive parent, it's a whole other thing to peer into a man's soul as he wrestles with God. *After They Are Yours* opens a window into the life of a father of an adoptive family and allows you to peek into his mind, seeing snapshots of and watching him grapple with his raw emotions. He's a husband, a protector and defender of his wife. Oh yes, he's a father, duty bound to raise up his children to live a disciplined life through discipleship, love and second chances. He's a man…strong yet weak. The power of his struggle beckons you to pray for the father. This book was a glimpse of how God fights for us and doesn't let go. I wanted to be their intercessor. *After They Are Yours* reminds us of the importance of having people who will wrap around adoptive families with support and prayer when a family says 'Yes' to God's call to adopt. It reinforces that God has called for a lifetime commitment when we adopt and that He will be faithful."

Dr. Sharen Ford, Program Director of Adoption & Orphan Care, Focus on the Family

"This book will be a blessed resource for all parents who have adopted or are considering adopting a child. It is rooted in sound theology and personal experience. The author is realistic about the unique and significant challenges faced by those who adopt ("adopt boldly with eyes wide open"), while also extolling the privilege of reflecting God's grace by seeking to rescue a child from darkness ("God enters into this abusive, oppressive family and removes us"). The greatest strength of this book is the transparent way in which the author tells his family's adoption story. He openly shares his own struggles and sins along with his family's experiences of God's grace and mercy. His insights will benefit all parents, not just those who have adopted."

Dr. Jim Newheiser, pastor, author, Director of the Institute of Biblical Counseling and Discipleship, founding member of the Fellowship of Independent Reformed Evangelicals

"Just as marriage is given to us by God and intended to reflect, however imperfectly, the relationship between Christ and His church, earthly adoption illustrates the glorious work of God's sovereign, gracious adoption of each of us into His family so that we may cry out "Abba, Father!" And just as marriage is a marred reflection due to our sinful condition, adoption is fraught with peril and pain along with the joy and gladness.

After They are Yours is a vivid, plain spoken picture of that joy and pain. Would that all the adoptive families I have worked with over the decades could have read this as part of the adoptive process! The book also presents a clear, Biblical teaching concerning a proper response to the difficulties which arise in every adoption and in fact in every parent's life.

My wife, Diane, and I have watched this joy and pain and

love lived out in the lives of Brian and Ariel and all three of our Borgman grandkids, and can testify to God's gracious faithfulness and provision for them, and to God's love of adoption, on earth as it is in heaven!

I highly recommend this very accessible, truthful picture of adoption."

Judge David Gamble, elder; President and Trustee of City of Refuge, Gardnerville, NV

"Too many people enter the adoption process with false hopes, images of grandeur, and rose-colored glasses about their future with an adopted child that too often are based on marketing and adoptive parents not sharing 'the rest of the story.' The consequences of such misguided beliefs and motives can be devastating to the adopted child and adoptive family. Thankfully, we now have *After They Are Yours* to protect well-intentioned, prospective parents from the perils of ignorance and prepare them for their future. Through his raw honesty, vulnerability, and insight, and with scriptural truths as his foundation, Borgman gives potential and current adoptive parents, and any other parents for that matter, an invaluable resource to ensure that they can enter into the life-changing world of adoption with eyes wide open."

Philip Darke, President of Providence World and co-author of *In Pursuit of Orphan Excellence*

"Brian invites us into his family's adoption journey with refreshingly raw honesty, where he articulates the very real challenges and very real joy found in the day-to-day 'after they are yours.'"

Andy Lehman, Vice President of Lifesong for Orphans and Founding Board Member of the Christian Alliance for Orphans & the Orphan Sunday campaign

"With the explosion of the orphan care movement among evangelicals in recent years, this book provides a timely, much needed perspective on the challenges often facing adoptive and foster parents. As Borgman takes readers on his family's journey of adoption, he does not hold back on some of his most personal struggles. While some of these anecdotes may be difficult to read, this transparent, gritty story highlights how God loves to take the messiest of situations and then transform them for his glory. This book provides a healthy dose of realism every prospective adoptive parent needs, followed by practical insights and the hope of redemption that is only found in the Gospel."

Matt Oettinger, Campus Elder/Orphan Care Ministry Leader of The Summit Church, Raleigh-Durham, NC

"Adoption, like missions for so many years before, has been sold to sincere disciples by romanticizing the calling. And as in missions many have flung themselves into the noble life-altering calling of adoption only to find themselves secretly wondering if they have been sold a bill of goods. The prince has turned into a toad. The good news is most refreshing to those who feel stuck in a bad story but are too ashamed and afraid to admit that reality is not that charming. Too often we unintentionally promote noble callings, like missions and adoption, with the lure of prosperity; not because we promise blessing, but because we do not honestly warn of difficulty. Brian Borgman's book is long overdue. He boldly unveils the secret too many are unwilling to discuss: adoption can be very, very hard. This will be a book that I will buy and hand out to many couples who with starry eyes plunged into the calling of adoption and are now in the full shock of difficulty. They, like Bunyan's Mr. Ready-to-halt will find in Pastor Borgman a Mr. Great-heart who tells them as the sincere and weary traveler was told, 'Your travel hither has been with difficulty, but that will make thy Rest the sweeter.'"

Bob Bixby, Lead Pastor of Redeemer Church, Fremont, CA

"*After They Are Yours* is a compelling acknowledgment that parenting adopted children can be uniquely challenging. Brian Borgman lets us step into his family's experience as he unashamedly shares the joys and difficulties of their adoption story. Pain and loss are an inescapable part of every adoption, and Borgman points us to the Gospel that provides both the framework and the fuel that families will need for the challenges that come. Grace and grit indeed; this is an excellent resource."

Stephen Story, Executive Director, Covenant Care Services

Table of Contents

CruciformPress

Our Books: Short and to the point—about 100 pages.
Clear. Concise. Helpful. Inspiring. Easy to read.
Solid authors. Gospel-focused. Local-church oriented.

Multiple formats: Print and the three top ebook formats.

Consistent Pricing: Every title the same low price.

Website Discounts:

Print Books (list price $9.99)

1-5 Books	$8.45 each
6-50 Books	$7.45 each
More than 50 Books	$6.45 each

Ebooks (list price $7.50)

Single Ebooks	$5.45 each
Bundles of 7 Ebooks	$35.00
Ebook Distribution Program	6 pricing levels

Subscription Options: If you choose, print books or
ebooks delivered to you on a schedule, at a discount.

Print Book Subscription *(list $9.99)*	$6.49 each
Ebook Subscription *(list $7.50)*	$3.99 each

After They Are Yours: The Grace and Grit of Adoption

Print / PDF ISBN: 978-1-936760-92-3
ePub ISBN: 978-1-936760-94-7
Mobipocket ISBN: 978-1-936760-93-0

Foreword

Romanticizing adoption is so easy and so tempting. Who doesn't approve of the idea of giving a child a loving home? Who doesn't want to see an orphan loved by a committed Christian family? When we primarily look at adoption as giving orphans homes, it's tempting to think of their placement in a home as the happy ending—the child who was without hope and home in the world now has a loving family. Yes, the day an orphan becomes a loved-on child in a permanent family is indeed happy. But let's never forget that the post-adoption journey always involves some suffering. Especially when the adopted child is older, that "happy ending" is often just the beginning of a much longer, difficult story—a story marked by struggles with attachment and bonding, and by visceral feelings of loneliness, resentment, anger, doubt, and regret. Love may often seem elusive, and is sometimes simply impossible. To borrow words from Isaiah 53:3, the post-adoption journey is frequently "acquainted with grief."

Having served with Together for Adoption for almost 7 years now, I have talked to many couples who began their adoption journeys with great anticipation and excitement, only to be met with behavioral and emotional issues that quickly moved them out of their depth. Every one of these couples went from feeling *hopeful* as parents to feeling *hopeless*. And often what makes this sense of hopelessness especially unbearable is feeling unsupported or misunder-stood by the local and larger Christian community.

For a great many adoptive families, the most difficult and longest part of the adoption journey is what happens after they are yours.

This is why I am extremely grateful for this new book. Brian Borgman is a husband, father, and pastor who has experienced both the beauty and brokenness of adoption. He wants to provide specific, tangible help to two kinds of families—those who struggle with "the hidden side of adoption," as well as prospective adoptive parents, so they may adopt boldly with eyes wide open, depending daily upon the unmatched grace of God in the grit of the adoption journey.

After They Are Yours is not watered down or sanitized. Brian writes with a raw, refreshing honesty and vulnerability, coupled with hope-giving biblical insight and courage. His use and application of Scripture is compelling and convincing. This is a book the Lord will use to bring many adoptive families through the deep, dark shadows that often accompany the journey on "the other side of adoption."

If you are a prospective adoptive parent, an adoptive family in the midst of post-adoption struggles, or someone who knows such families, Brian wrote this book for you. As you read , my hope is that you will know and experience the grace of God the Father in the grit of adoption.

Dan Cruver
President, Together for Adoption
Editor and co-author of *Reclaiming Adoption: Missional Living through the Rediscovery of Abba Father*

INTRODUCTION

Why I Wrote This Book

This book has numerous origins, but perhaps the most catalytic was a conversation I had with Eli Perez from *Family Life Today*. I had traveled to Little Rock, Arkansas to be interviewed for their radio program, and Eli was assigned to take me to lunch. As we sat in P.F. Chang's he made a simple, sincere request.

"Tell me about your family."

"Well, I have three children, Ashley, Zach, and Alex." As I went on about my kids, I got around to Alex's athletic exploits. "He is a Babe Ruth All-Star. He not only is a terrific pitcher with a frightening fastball, he can hit the ball a mile. He has been a varsity basketball player since he was a freshman. He is a leading rebounder and scorer. He is All-league and team MVP. He gets under the basket and knows how to bang bodies, box out and score and rebound. Oh, he also won state in discus and placed in shot put. It was the first year he ever threw."

Eli looked at me and asked the inevitable question, "How big is he?"

"He is 6'1" and weighs 210 pounds."

Looking at me he could tell something was amiss.

I laughed and said, "Alex is adopted. He didn't get his size or athletic ability from me!"

Eli began asking questions about how long Alex has been in our family and what our adoption experience has been like.

I told him, "His mom and I have often talked about writing a book, *The Other Side of Adoption*. It has been really tough. Years of blessings *and* deep struggles."

Eli then told me stories of families he has known who also have struggled with adoptions. Some of those stories involved real tragedies. He encouraged me to pursue the idea of writing such a book. "I think something like that needs to be written."

Since that time, not only has Alex grown, but my sense of the need for this book has grown. Even while ministering in a closed country in the Far East, I was asked by the pastor to sit down with three families who were all going through adoptive family struggles. I listened to their heartache and trials and tried to offer some biblical counsel and lessons learned through personal experience. Although the culture was vastly different, the problems and challenges were the same.

Thankful for Adoption

I have served as pastor at a church in Nevada since 1993, and one thing I am so very thankful for is the wonderful emphasis our church gives to adoption. You could say that our church specializes in adoption. One of our vital ministries is the City of Refuge, a home operated by a couple in the church. Through this ministry we take care of unwed pregnant moms who have made the choice to give their babies life. We also facilitate the choice by some of these moms to give their baby *a* life through adoption. So many heart-warming stories have come from the City of Refuge, stories of babies saved from abortion and adopted into loving families. In addition, many families in our church have adopted children. One family in particular adopted a special needs baby and is looking to adopt again. Another family recently completed an international adoption of multiple children from a very dark and dangerous country. These families are heroes.

I am also thankful for books like Russell Moore's *Adopted for Life* and conferences like *Together for Adoption*. Even the movie *The Blind Side* has contributed to a resurgence of interest in adoption in our society and especially in the church. At the time of this writing, a recent edition of WORLD Magazine featured several inspiring stories of adoption. For society to see the beauty of adoption is a good thing, and for the church to be actively engaged in adoption is a powerful testimony to true religion. "Religion that is pure and undefiled before God, the Father, is this: to visit orphans and widows in their affliction, and to keep oneself unstained from the world" (James 1:27). Adoption is an expression of pure and undefiled religion.

I love adoption for three reasons. The first has two interlocking components: adoption is a redemptive theme in the Bible that extols God's marvelous love; and adoption is a viable alternative to the tragic sin of abortion. As pro-lifers, we cannot afford merely to express our opposition to abortion. We must also be out front in offering real alternatives to women who experience an unplanned pregnancy. Adoption is one of those alternatives. To say "no" to abortion is to give the baby life. To say "yes" to adoption when the mother is not prepared to keep the child is to give the baby *a* life.

The second reason I love adoption is because as Christians we should reflect the compassion of our heavenly Father by seeking to bring relief to those who are suffering. When a Christian couple seeks to rescue children from orphanages—especially from countries where the living conditions may be especially inhumane—they are manifesting the compassionate heart of God who delights to relieve the suffering of the afflicted.

Finally, I love adoption because my wife and I are adoptive parents. We know the great joys of adoption, but we also know the other side—the pain and tears, the anger and frustration. We know the perplexity of wondering, "Is this really worth it?" and the shame of having even asked the question. We know the thrill of watching Alex excel, and the guilt and heartbreak of erupting with an anger that seems to make all the joys and thrills evaporate in a moment.

Discouraging Words

Some will read that last paragraph and think, "Well, that's not just adoptive parents; that describes many parents." True enough. All kids are sinners. I've heard many times there isn't "supposed" to be any difference in the parenting experience between adopted and natural children. And certainly there are adoptive families in which the children assimilate beautifully, where the parental love is noble and unreserved. But there are also many godly, spiritually mature parents who struggle with a difficult adopted child, who feel the distance and detachment of the child's affections and suffer the tensions of a weak or non-existent parent-child bond. For those of us who have lived it, we know there can be a difference.

This is why words such as the following—well-meaning, and from an outstanding, milestone book on Christian adoption—can so easily discourage and disserve struggling adoptive parents.

> You'll hear often from adopting parents who immediately blame all behavioral and discipline problems on the circumstance of the adoption. Sometimes parents will panic about "attachment disorder" because the child is mischievous or strong-willed.
>
> In the vast majority of cases, however, parents are simply identifying the normal range of differences in children, or they're blaming bad behavior or uninformed parenting on a "syndrome." This isn't unique to adoption....There may indeed be factors involved in misbehavior, but in the vast majority of instances, a child's misbehavior is explained by Genesis, not genes; by Eden, not adoption.
>
> People speak of rearing "adopted children" with hushed tones and raised eyebrows, as though this task is not for the faint of heart. They speak of the trials of "adopted" children with their identity crises and

hidden hurts, as though one is predestined for misery because of adoption itself....

The reality, though, is that in most ways parenting is parenting, and growing up is growing up. It's always hard. Some unique challenges go along with adoption—challenges related to finding a sense of belonging, to discipline and discipleship, to answering questions about origins. Count these as all joy.[1]

It's not my intention to dissect this statement at any length. There is obviously a measure of truth here—truth that some adoptive parents do need to receive. Recently, however, when I read these words to a group in a workshop at a biblical counseling conference, I heard the sighs and saw the hurt. And I know why.

To give just two examples, Reactive Attachment Disorder and Fetal Alcohol Syndrome are deeply painful realities that many adoptive families must live with. Words like those quoted above can suggest to struggling parents that such conditions are, if not quite imaginary, then either inconsequential or exceedingly rare. This only adds to the shame, increases the silence of real suffering, and discourages parental attempts to uncover potential underlying factors. Instead of trying to learn about the condition of an adopted child, adoptive parents—especially Christians—often think they are bad parents, ineffective disciplinarians, or even failures. They can feel hopeless, not to mention isolated from and unsupported by the very community that ought to understand.

Those who do learn about attachment disorders or

Fetal Alcohol Syndrome may feel ashamed, as if making excuses when trying to explain their challenges. My wife and I have been there and we know of many other adoptive parents who have as well. To these parents the shared experiences are familiar and the hurt, isolation, and sense of shame are real.

Comforting Words

For years it seemed as though very few materials dealt head-on with the struggles of adoptive families. Thankfully, that seems to be changing.

> For all its beauty, adoption also has significant challenges… Although you are doing a wonderful thing, you must recognize that children were meant to live with their natural parents. When children are raised by those who aren't their natural parents, there will be struggles and difficulties. *Parenting an adopted child is often harder than parenting your natural child. Your adopted child deals with significant personal issues that your natural child never has to deal with.*[2]

I was so glad and relieved when I first read these words a few years ago.

Like any other difficult journey in the Christian life, the journey of adoption will always benefit from honesty and transparency. Many adoptive parents I talk to—and I talk to many—often feel misunderstood by family and friends. They frequently feel judged because they are "too hard" on the child. Or they hear, "He behaves himself just fine when he is with us…" Often we are made to feel as though we are whining if we talk about our challenges.

So let me make this clear from the beginning—this book is the story of our challenges as adoptive parents. I don't believe any of it qualifies as whining, but you can judge that for yourself. Certainly the experiences of some adoptive parents have been much better than ours. For others, the experience has been far worse. I don't claim that what we've been through grants us any special authority or status, but I do think our story will resonate with a great many adoptive parents.

• • •

A Brief Aside

All struggles in the Christian life share the same root cause, the same hope, the same source of strength, and the same ultimate resolution. All of us who have been spiritually adopted by the Father can be strengthened when we see how God has worked in the lives of other struggling Christians, regardless of the nature of those struggles. For this reason, I believe that what you read in this book can be inspiring, encouraging, and helpful to you—even if you are not involved in adoption in any way. If that's you, I encourage you to read on. Listen in as I talk directly to adoptive parents; no one will mind. Take a look at our lives and the struggles we've faced. They won't be exactly like yours, but the grace, mercy, and strength we have found in God in the midst of it all is exactly what you can find in your abiding challenges. We share the same Father, the same Savior, the same Spirit, and we all live in the same fallen world. In a very real way, our struggles are yours, and yours are ours. We're in this together.

● ● ●

I hope that what I have to say in this book, informed and shaped by Scripture, will be helpful to parents like us who struggle. But know that you'll find no special solution here, no offer of peace and freedom that will solve all your problems in this life. All I can offer you is my experience with Scripture. Through its truth and guidance, through conviction and encouragement, Scripture has been my lifeline to God. It has helped me immeasurably in all our struggles, and in very specific, tangible ways. The truth of Scripture, and our experience of interacting with it and receiving encouragement from it, lies at the heart of our story as adoptive parents. Certainly I have nothing of value to tell you apart from what Scripture has done for us and through us in the midst of our struggles. In this book, I want to show you how Scripture has been our support and help—because I know it can be yours as well, regardless of your circumstances.

In the end, I hope this book accomplishes two purposes. The first is to encourage families who struggle with "the other side of adoption" or what happens "after they are yours." The second is to encourage prospective adoptive parents to adopt boldly with eyes wide open, knowing both the challenges that may lie ahead and that there is grace from God, sufficient grace, to give them all they need to do something so incredibly God-like. A friend of mine, an adoptive parent of four, wrote, "As a parent you need truth. The quicker you know the truth, the quicker you can adjust your expectations and start advocating for your child. Not knowing is dangerous. Too many adoptive parents are living, parenting, and problem solving in the dark—or at least in a heavy fog bank."

May our heavenly Father, who adopted us by his grace, use this book to equip parents "after they are yours."

One
FROM CONVICTION TO FOSTER CARE

Our Story, Part One

I am going to speak transparently about our struggles with Alex, so there are two things you should be aware of. First, Alex knows I will share some of the more painful events of our lives and he is OK with that, so please don't think I'm talking behind his back. Second, I am writing mostly out of our failures, not our successes. My wife, Ariel, and I learned way too late some of the lessons described in this book. Some of the stories reveal our sin. We are OK with that because we are sinners who have been forgiven by a loving Savior and by Alex. Because I'm a pastor, some might think I have a reputation to protect. But I'm not concerned that some of our stories may raise eyebrows. I am not looking for a call to a bigger church, and I am secure in my relationship with the family of Grace Community Church, so I am going to let the clay show. My family and I live in the real world of sin and failure, and for these reasons and many more we are thankful for the grace of God in Jesus Christ.

How It All Started

My wife, Ariel, and I have always been strongly pro-life. We believe abortion is murder, our national tragedy and crisis, and the worst form of oppression and injustice in the world today. Like many pro-life people we support our local community pregnancy center as well as pro-life candidates. But something was missing. We thought we could do more. We knew a man in a neighboring church who worked for Koinonia Ministries. This is a Christian ministry that helps train people, especially Christians, to be foster parents.[3] The ministry also serves as a liaison with local child and family services in helping place foster children. We wanted to get involved. Helping out a child in desperate need of love, care, and safety seemed to be fully consistent with our pro-life principles.

"We Would Like to Help"

We went through the initial training, then through additional training to qualify as therapeutic foster parents who could take care of special-needs children. At times the training was daunting. Horror stories abounded. But we were committed, confident that this was a way to serve God. Helping a child in need was a good thing and we knew God would help us.

Then came the day when the state social worker came to our house for our final interview. He asked whether we spanked our own children. I answered, "Yes. Is that a problem? We understand we cannot spank the foster children."

"Oh no. No problem. Just making some notes."

He went on. "I notice you seem to be very religious. How many times a week do you go to church?"

"Well, I am the pastor. I am technically at church every day. Is there a problem?"

"No. No problem. What other kind of religious activities do you do outside of church?"

"We have family devotions."

"How often?"

"Every day."

"What do those consist of?"

"Well, we read the Bible or a book together. We pray. And we sing. I am not sure why you are asking these questions."

"Don't worry Mr. Borgman, I am just trying to get a feel for your home environment."

When the social worker left I had a sinking feeling in my stomach. I said to Ariel, "I bet they deny us."

"They can't deny us because we are Christians and spank our own kids," she said.

After the two-week period for review and approval we still had not heard anything. Another week went by and I called Koinonia to express our concerns. I was assured they would look into it. Koinonia called back and said there were just some delays. Another two weeks passed and this time Koinonia initiated contact with the state. After some relentless probing, Koinonia was told the social worker noted that we "used corporal punishment on our biological children and were excessively religious." The social worker recommended that we be denied foster parent status.

The Koinonia director could not believe what he was hearing. He protested. He appealed to the fact that spanking your biological children is not against the law. He argued that we had gone through the training and had a stable marriage, family, and home life. He reminded them that we were the very kind of people the state was looking for to fill a huge need for the perpetual demands for safe foster homes. None of his arguments prevailed.

We concluded that the Lord had closed this door. Our consciences were clear. We had made our plans, we had done our best, and we knew our hearts were in the right place. We had prayed that God would give us favor, and we believed he had directed our steps (Proverbs 16:9). Yet the door seemed to be shut. God's ways are certainly not our ways.

"A Tough One"

About a month later I received a call from the state. "Mr. Borgman, we have a 20-month-old little boy who needs immediate foster care."

"I'm sorry, we weren't approved for foster care," I said.

"Well, Mr. Borgman, I have a paper right here that says you have provisional approval to care for children up to 24 months old."

"When was that dated?"

"Today. Are you interested?"

"Let me call you back."

I called Koinonia. Ariel was excited. I was apprehensive. The director was upset because the state had broken two matters of protocol. First, the state is supposed to contact Koinonia for placements with Koinonia-trained foster parents. Second, there was no age limitation in the approval process. To be trained for therapeutic care was to be eligible for children of any age who were in need. Knowing our desire to care for a child, he contacted the state to inquire about this particular child.

The director's words are forever embedded in my mind. "Brian, this little guy is a tough one. He is 20 months old. He has a 36-month-old brother. The state needs to separate them. They are violent together. Brian, he has been in four homes in six weeks. No one seems to be able to handle him. It will be a tough assignment to break you in on. Don't feel bad if you pass on this one. There will be others."

"Let me talk to Ariel—we need to pray about it."

I told my wife about this little boy and, before I could even say, "Let's pray about it," she told me, "This is the kind of child we need to help. I think we should say *yes.*" That was it. I knew resistance was futile! Within two hours a kind and friendly case worker brought Alex to our home.

Alex had blonde hair and blue eyes and looked like a 20-month-old action figure. He had muscles and a little six-pack. He was quiet and observant for the first week, except when he ate. When we put him in his high chair to feed him he dug in with both hands. He knew what it was to go without a meal—or two or three—so he tried to cram as much food into his little mouth as possible. Ariel put a bowl of fruit on the bottom shelf of the refrigerator and told him he could eat anytime (something we learned in our training). We were heartbroken at his plight and delighted to be able to help. That was the first week. An excerpt from Ariel's journal on 7/2/97 reads, "Alex played well today and tonight with Ash and Zach. He smiled, laughed, ate well, played well with toys, looked at a couple books, had a bottle at 8:30 pm, and was tucked into bed at 8:45. He went right to sleep, happy."

"Happy" wasn't the word to describe the second week. The second week started with teeth marks. Alex decided to bite Zach, who is three years older than Alex. Alex also decided that wearing his cereal would be more fun than eating it. How could he eat like a ravenous zombie and then dump cereal on his head? He threw tantrums, screamed, and was an all-around disruptive force. Ariel was exhausted and I realized why he had been in four homes in six weeks. Ariel wrote, "A long afternoon of testing! Lots of biting (he bit both Ash and Zach). Lots of hitting and pushing. Ash and Zach went to evening service with Dad, I stayed home and put Alex to bed. I need a break. I'm beat."

With strict limitations on how we could discipline, we felt at a loss to know what to do. "Time out" was a bust because he would occupy himself by destroying something. One morning Alex dumped the cereal and sticky milk on his head again. Ariel, thinking quickly, took him into the bathroom and ran a cold bath. He screamed and squirmed as she bathed him in the cold water. From that point on, the cereal stayed in the bowl.

Then we went on a family vacation eastward across the United States. We drove. In a mini-van. What were we thinking?

Heading for New Jersey, we checked into a roadside hotel in Salt Lake City. Our room was on the third floor, and as I went back down to the van to get the rest of the luggage, Ariel opened the windows to air out the room. While unloading the van I heard Alex yelling, "Daddy! Hi, Daddy!" As I looked up, he was standing on the windowsill, pounding on the screen which was in the process of falling out. As my heart burst out of my chest I hollered up to Ariel, and Alex was rescued. That's when we realized that Alex had no fear.

Later in New Jersey, while leaving a K-Mart, Alex and Zach wanted to ride those little toy cars that rock back and forth. We put in the quarters and let them ride. When Zach's ride was over he got off. When Alex's ride was over he stayed in the car, trying violently to make it keep rocking. I told him it was time to go. He looked at me without a word and went back to rocking the car. After a couple more commands, "Alex, get down, we need to leave," he was blatantly ignoring me. This was a shock. I was not used to being ignored by my children.

I motioned to Ariel that we should walk off a little ways. We grabbed the other two kids and said, "Bye, Alex." He didn't say a word, just kept trying to force that car to go again. We walked further. While he was never out of our sight, he never looked at us once. He never called for us. We stood there for ten minutes in stunned silence; he was completely indifferent to our absence. He only cared about the car. We began to understand the meaning of "reactive attachment disorder." There would be many other episodes like this one.

Alex was diagnosed with Fetal Alcohol Syndrome and Attention Deficit Disorder. He was also delayed in speech. We decided that we would not let these diagnoses define him or excuse him. We did our best to love and help him. As time went on, Alex improved. In spite of some improvement, we were never without Alex-generated chaos or destruction. Life was always interesting with Alex.

Two
FROM FOSTER CHILD TO SON

Our Story, Part Two

One day there was a knock on the door. To my great surprise it was a fellow seminary student I had graduated with in 1993. We had been Greek study buddies. We really hadn't seen each other in 20 years, but he was up at Tahoe for a family vacation and decided to stop in.

The visit turned serious as I asked him about his family. He and his wife had been childless for nine years. They tried everything to help them with fertility, but nothing worked. They concluded that God wanted them to grow their family through adoption, so they adopted four half-siblings. Since the adoption they had encountered challenges that at times shook them deeply. He told me, "We began to realize that foster care has hidden strengths that adoption lacks. Mostly that has to do with permanency. If things get too bad with a foster child you can always request they be removed from your home. And there is a sense you were trying to help someone else's child and it just didn't work out. It is sad but doesn't really rock your core."

For us, things were certainly tough with Alex. We were tired and frustrated, and so often we felt out of our depth. Frankly, if Ariel had said, "We tried to help this little boy, but it is too much," I would not have resisted. But I am married to a stubborn, loving wife who does not know how to give up. She was committed to Alex, her motherly instinct had kicked in, and she was on a mission from God. I think Alex could have burned the house down and she still would have refused to call Child and Family Services!

In the words of another mom, "There are days when I'm completely overwhelmed, and I wonder if we made the right decision....If we really knew what we were getting into, none of us do it in the moment. But I would do it over and over again.... God...doesn't make mistakes."[4]

That was Ariel. She was confident that God had a purpose for having Alex in our home. She was confident that God had called us to love him. Yes, it was hard. Yes, she was overwhelmed. But she never wavered in what she believed was God's plan for Alex and for us.

Every month, a Koinonia worker and a state social worker came to check on Alex. One particular check-up stands out to us. Alex's case worker went through the regular questions with us, and then she spoke to Alex (which never yielded much information). She closed her notebook and looked at us with a smile and said, "Alex has done so well. You guys should be really proud of yourselves. In fact, his improvement is so remarkable that the office has decided that he does not need therapeutic foster care anymore."

"What exactly does that mean?" I asked.

"Well, Alex will be moved to a lower-level-care foster home."

Ariel fought back tears and anger. I was incredulous. I am generally mild-mannered. I don't like returning items to the store because I don't want to be critical or embarrassed. I won't send undercooked food back at a restaurant; I would rather risk salmonella than voice an objection. But on that day I tossed mild manners out the window.

"Are you kidding me? Are you actually telling us that since we did such a good job with Alex and he has improved that now he must be moved? That is insanity. You told us he has attachment disorder and now you want to move him out of our home after he has started to feel safe and that he belongs?"

"Well, that's the policy. Alex no longer needs the level of care you are licensed to provide."

"Then we are no longer therapeutic foster parents, we are just ordinary lower-level foster parents."

"Mr. Borgman, it doesn't work that way." And with that, she left.

We were devastated. We knew the state was close to making a decision on whether to pursue terminating the parental rights of Alex's biological parents. If they did, he would be placed for adoption. Ariel and I had discussed adopting Alex, and she was much more in favor of the idea than I was, but in any event taking him out of our home at this point seemed ridiculous. We immediately contacted Koinonia and put the prayer warriors in our church to work, storming the throne of grace.

"I don't know how you did it," said the case worker a few days later, "but you are no longer therapeutic foster parents and Alex is staying in your home."

We asked about Alex's birth mom and what Child and Family Services were planning to do. She told us CFS was planning to start proceedings shortly, so we immediately indicated that we wanted to adopt Alex. I wasn't necessarily convinced this was right for our family, but Ariel felt certain it was. Eventually, I came to change my mind. More accurately, God changed my mind. I was not all that happy with *how* God changed my mind, but he did. Honestly, at times, in the eye of the storm, both Ariel and I have questioned whether we made the right decision. And whenever we do, God reminds us that Alex is a Borgman by sovereign appointment.

At first we wanted an open adoption, one in which the birth parents can interact with the child within certain limitations. We knew that because of drugs and alcohol Alex's birth parents were unable to take care of him, but we couldn't see cutting off all contact through a closed adoption. We met informally at a park with the birth mom, the social worker, and Alex's brother. The boys played while we explained to the birth mom that we wanted to help her. Although we had come to love Alex, reunification was important to us. Nothing would ever change the fact that she carried Alex in her womb for nine months and birthed him. However, if she didn't feel like she could raise him or couldn't get her life together, we would be happy to adopt him. It was a cordial meeting, but it didn't take us long to see that she would not be able to care for him.

Later we met formally with Alex's birth mom, birth grandmother, and a social worker to discuss the terms of the open adoption. The state had informed her that they would begin termination of her parental rights, but if she relinquished those rights and worked out an open adoption agreement, she would have opportunity to maintain some level of contact with Alex.

But at the meeting, almost her first words were, "I would like to have him every other weekend. We could switch the holidays…" Somehow, the birth mom thought we were there to work out a joint custody arrangement.

"Hold on a minute." I rudely interrupted. I said to the social worker, "Would you please explain to her that this is not joint custody, it is an adoption. That means that once a year we send a school picture, that perhaps on birthdays she can send a card, and *maybe* once a year we can arrange a visit."

Looking as if she had been hit in the forehead with a brick, she looked incredulously at the social worker and asked, "Is that true?"

"Yes, that's true."

There was a long, awkward silence. Then the grandmother spoke up. "You know, they are good people. They love Alex. You should do this. It would be good for him."

She replied with a simple yet defiantly reluctant, "Okay."

We then discussed the terms of the open adoption, and the state set the court date for the birth mom to relinquish her parental rights. After that court date she would sign the open adoption agreement. But as we left the

meeting that day I had an uneasy feeling. Could the birth
mom really have thought she was going to get overnight
visits every other weekend? Could she really have
thought Alex would spend Thanksgiving with her and
then Christmas with us? As the court date approached,
Ariel and I were apprehensive. As it turned out, we had
every reason to be.

When the court date came we drove to Yerington,
Nevada, and met at the courthouse, a grand old brick
structure with the Ten Commandments on an indestruc-
tible plaque out front. We were all supposed to sign the
open-adoption papers before our appointed time with
the judge, so we had arrived early. Birth mom was late.
As birth mom and grandmother drove up, Ariel and I
stood outside with the social worker, one of the CFS
department heads, and the original case worker who had
brought Alex to us. When they got out of the car I could
smell alcohol. Birth mom blurted out, "Where's Alex?"
We explained that it wasn't appropriate for him to be there.
She huffed and walked into the courthouse. Clearly there
was going to be trouble.

We were all rushed upstairs by the Assistant District
Attorney and put into a tiny office. Birth mom sat at the
desk, her mother squeezed in behind her left shoulder,
the social worker behind her right. Ariel sat in front of
the desk, and for lack of room I stood in the doorway.
The social worker politely said, "We don't want to rush
through this, but we do need to be downstairs in court in
less than 15 minutes."

The social worker then patiently went through the

document which would terminate birth mom's parental rights. She read each line aloud, asking questions and explaining phrases as necessary. At one point she asked if birth mom was married when Alex was born. Birth mom answered abruptly with a "Yes." Her mother said calmly, "You were not married when Alex was born." A mini-shouting match erupted in the tiny room. Grandmother quickly backed down. Then the social worker came to a clause indicating that the agreement was irrevocable.

The social worker asked, "Do you understand 'irrevocable'"?

"What the hell is irrevocable?" was birth mom's irritated reply.

"It means you are signing something that cannot be changed."

In a fit of anger, birth mom took the pen and violently slashed and stabbed the paper, tearing it to pieces. She stood up and pushed her way past the social worker toward the door. Stopping inches away from me, she leaned into my face and, with rage in her voice, said, "Now I know what it's like to be screwed by a Baptist." With that she stormed out of the room, with her mother calling after her.

We went downstairs where everyone was anxiously awaiting our arrival since we were next on the docket. The ADA asked where birth mom was. Before an answer could be given, I spoke up. "I know we were here to sign papers for an open adoption. But after what I just saw, I am withdrawing our offer of an open adoption. I do not believe that birth mom's presence in Alex's life or our life would be good for any of us." To our surprise the social worker said, "I agree." The original case worker expressed his agreement, noting that the environment he took Alex from was one of the worst he had ever seen. The ADA said, "No problem, we can begin termination today."

Ariel and I thought that was it, but then court began. The judge entered and we all stood, birth mom's attorney all by himself, with grandmother in the row behind him.

"You may be seated," said the judge. "Counsel, where is birth mom?"

"Well your honor, the person screaming out in the lobby, that would be her."

"Is she going to come in?"

Grandmother said, "I will go get her."

Soon, birth mom stormed into the courtroom, threw her purse on the floor, plopped down in the chair next to her attorney and said, "Where do I sign? I am ready to sign."

The judge gave a word of warning and the ADA said, "Your honor, we are no longer pursuing an open adoption, but rather we are going to terminate birth mom's parental rights."

Birth mom began asking her attorney what was going on. The judge told her to be quiet. The ADA went on. "Your honor, I have been informed by Child and Family Services that the Borgmans have changed their minds about an open adoption due to birth mom's erratic behavior today."

The judge asked the CFS representative if they were in agreement. "We are, your honor." The judge warned birth mom and her attorney again, set a new date, and… dismissed us. Huh?

Ariel and I looked at each other in bewilderment. What was this? As soon as we left the courtroom we asked the social worker why the judge hadn't terminated birth mom's parental rights. "Well, it is not that easy. We will see what happens in three months."

The next year and a half was a roller coaster. We would show up to court, wondering if today would be the day. Sometimes birth mom would show up, sometimes she wouldn't. The court kept giving her stipulations: permanent housing for six months, a steady job, AA or NA meetings every week, parenting classes and sobriety. On one occasion she reported that she had attended a few meetings and had a job. Other than that, no progress. Still, the court kept granting her more time.⁵

Finally the day came when the judge signed the termination papers, thus allowing the adoption to begin. We went through the home study again. We filled out more paperwork. We secured a wonderful attorney in our area who loves doing adoptions.

The pieces were finally coming together. Alex was going to be a Borgman.

Simply Our Son

By the time all of this inched towards its conclusion, Alex had reached school age. Like Ashley and Zach before him, we sent Alex to our local public school for Kindergarten. But unlike Ashley, who shed rivers of tears that first day, Alex took off running without knowing exactly where he was going. Zach had at least known where he was going when *he* took off.

Although he was well-behaved at school and church, he continued to be a terror at home. It didn't make sense to us. We concluded that if he could control himself at school or church or a friend's house, he should also be able to control himself at home. As Emily Belz recently wrote, "Children with post-adoption issues can be well-behaved toward people outside their family."[6] This is a reality that foster and adoptive parents know, yet often do not understand.

At home, Alex was destructive. He was frequently defiant and disobedient. He fought with his brother and sister constantly. He would throw tantrums. He would endanger himself by running away from us in parking lots. And there was that constant sense of detachment. One minute sitting on my lap cuddling, the next minute throwing a tantrum. One minute telling his mom he loved her, the next defying the simplest commands.

One Saturday, Ariel and the kids came to visit me at the church. As we were getting ready to leave, Alex and Zach were riding skateboards in the church parking lot. Ashley and Zach got into the van, but Alex refused. He ignored us and continued riding. I told him he had one last chance to obey, but he ignored me again. I shut the van door and started to drive off.

Ashley and Zach started crying and begged me not to leave him. Since we live in a rural area and nobody was around, I assured them I was just going around the block. Ariel and I watched Alex through our mirrors, but he never looked up. He just rode his skateboard. When we came back around the other side of the building, he was still riding, unconcerned that we had driven away. I had to physically put him in the van against his will. It seemed that any directive, any command, made him angry.

In spite of the struggles, the happy day came. On November 7, 2000, while America was voting and then waiting for election results, we were in the court of Dave Gamble. Dave is one of my dearest friends. He is an elder in our church and like a grandpa to my kids. He and his wife, Diane, have a huge heart for adoption. They are the founders of the home I mentioned earlier called the City of Refuge. Dave loves signing legal papers that change the status of a child.

Dave sat behind the bench in his black robe. Diane was holding balloons, and other dear friends were also in the courtroom. Our attorney explained to the group what was happening, and the social worker seemed impressed with the outpouring of love and support.

And there we sat with a little boy we had grown to love. There was joy, but there was also trepidation. Although we did not second guess our decision, I knew we had a tough road in front of us. Then Dave said something profound, "Brian and Ariel, you must understand that Alex is no longer your foster son. He is not even your adopted son. He is simply your son."

Then Dave had Alex come up and sit on his lap behind the bench. He gave Alex the gavel and let Alex adjourn the court. It was a beautiful day. Pictures of that day adorn our hallway, and I frequently stop and look back on the day of Alex's adoption.

We had a big party for Alex. There were so many people and so many presents. Something wonderful had happened and I knew it. My wife's love and persistence and prayers had brought Alex's foster care time to an end. He was now legally a Borgman.

When we were filling out the final paperwork, I asked Alex, then age 5, what he wanted his middle name to be. I told him that he could keep his middle name or use his original last name as his middle name. Or, he could take the middle name Zach and I share, which is also my father's name, "Steven." Without hesitation, he said he wanted to be called "Alexander Steven Borgman." He had his identity. He belonged. Alex was "simply our son." I thought that would give him a sense of security, but I had a lot to learn.

Three
THE DOCTRINE OF ADOPTION

"Daddy, are you preaching on adoption again?"

"Yes, Alex. I am going to preach on adoption again. Is that okay with you?"

"Yes. I like it when you preach about adoption because you talk about my adoption."

"That is because your adoption is such a wonderful picture of what God does for us when he adopts us into his family."

When I preached through Ephesians in our church, not long after Alex became a Borgman, I spent a tremendous amount of time on how "he predestined us for adoption as sons through Jesus Christ" (1:5). And when I have opportunity to preach in other places, I often preach on the doctrine of adoption. Invariably, I find that people are deeply moved by the truth of how God adopts us and what implications that has for us.

There are many fine books available now about the theology of adoption,[7] and I would encourage you to read them. In this chapter, we will explore briefly those theological truths that have deepened and shaped my own understanding of adoption.

A Biblical Truth

Adoption is a biblical truth. In fact, it is a central redemptive truth in the New Testament. As J. I. Packer has provocatively written: "Our understanding of Christianity cannot be better than our grasp of adoption."[8]

Adoption is an act of God's grace to us through the Lord Jesus Christ. God brings us into his family and makes us his own. Through Christ, we are given all the legal rights and privileges of God's children. All Christians, then, whether called to adopt children or not, should know and love this doctrine.

Scholars debate whether the theology of adoption has Old Testament roots or whether it is an adaptation of the Greco-Roman practice. The concept certainly has some Old Testament connections, though: God spoke of Israel as his firstborn son (Exodus 4:22), and in Hosea 11:1 God again identified Israel as his son. Romans 9:2–5 lists Israel's redemptive privileges, which include adoption: "They are Israelites, and to them belong the adoption" (v 4).

But whatever roots are growing in the Old Testament soil, the theme of adoption receives its full development by Paul in the New Testament. In Paul's writings, adoption is a vital part of our redemption. Although there is the pervasive truth that we are God's children through the work of Christ (e.g., John 1:12–13 and 1 John 2:29–3:1), the word "adoption" is unique to Paul. He uses it in three passages.

For you did not receive the spirit of slavery to fall
back into fear, but you have received the Spirit
of adoption as sons, by whom we cry, "Abba!
Father!"…And not only the creation, but we
ourselves, who have the firstfruits of the Spirit, groan
inwardly as we wait eagerly for adoption as sons, the
redemption of our bodies. (Romans 8:15, 23)

But when the fullness of time had come, God sent
forth his Son, born of woman, born under the law,
to redeem those who were under the law, so that we
might receive adoption as sons. And because you
are sons, God has sent the Spirit of his Son into our
hearts, crying, "Abba! Father!" So you are no longer
a slave, but a son, and if a son, then an heir through
God. (Galatians 4:4–7)

Blessed be the God and Father of our Lord Jesus
Christ, who has blessed us in Christ with every
spiritual blessing in the heavenly places, even as he
chose us in him before the foundation of the world,
that we should be holy and blameless before him. In
love he predestined us for adoption as sons through
Jesus Christ, according to the purpose of his will, to
the praise of his glorious grace, with which he has
blessed us in the Beloved. (Ephesians 1:3–6)

The word the ESV translates "adoption as sons"
is one word in Greek, one word with two concepts
wrapped up in it: adoption and sonship. Some transla-

tions emphasize one idea or the other (the NASB and ESV bring out both), but both concepts are present and are vitally important. Adoption is the divine act of God's grace, and sonship is the result of God's act. Put another way, sonship is the status God bestows through his gracious act of adoption.

All three passages bring into focus the wonderful grace of God in adoption. Furthermore, they tell us that adoption is a Trinitarian work. It is the plan of the Father (Ephesians 1:5), and it rightly relates us to God as our Father (Romans 8:15, Galatians 4:6–7). Adoption is the result of the Son's accomplished work of redemption (Galatians 4:4–5, Ephesians 1:5). And adoption becomes a reality for us when the Holy Spirit, as the Spirit of adoption, applies the Son's work of redemption to us (Romans 8:15, Galatians 4:6).

Adoption is Redemptive, Legal, and Relational

Though only used by Paul and only in the three passages quoted above, the word translated "adoption as sons" does some heavy theological work. Paul uses this term to concisely communicate beautiful truths about how God redeems sinners, makes them his legal heirs, and then enjoys a precious relationship with them.

"Adoption as sons" is a redemptive term. God's adoption of us equals redemption from slavery to sonship (Galatians 4:7). We were born as slaves to sin and slaves of the devil. Life in the devil's family is always slavery. But God enters into this abusive, oppressive situation and removes us. He then brings us into his own family where there is glorious redemption and freedom. No longer is our father the harsh taskmaster; rather, our Father is *Abba*.

"Adoption as sons" is also a legal term. In adoption, God grants to us the full rights, privileges, and immunities appropriate to his sons and daughters. He legally confers the status of sonship on those who formerly belonged to the domain of darkness (Colossians 1:13). We fully become "heirs of God and fellow heirs with Christ" (Romans 8:17).

Remember the story about Judge Gamble signing the papers that made Alex a Borgman? Here's more of what he said just after signing: "Brian and Ariel, you must understand that Alex is no longer your foster son. He is not even your adopted son. He is simply your son, entitled to all the benefits and affection and legal rights as if he had been born your son. Ashley and Zach, Alex is not your foster brother, nor is he your adopted brother. He is simply your little brother."

This is what our heavenly Father does with us…with one huge difference. In spiritual adoption, God serves as both judge and father. After he makes the legal declaration of sonship, God steps out from behind the bench, as it were, and embraces us because he is our Father.

"Adoption as sons" is a relational term. Perhaps it seems obvious that once God is our Father, we are now sons and daughters, but this truth has far-reaching implications. Paul emphasized this aspect of adoption when he described how the Holy Spirit comes into our lives and makes that Father-child relationship real to us so that we

cry out "Abba! Father!" (Romans 8:15, Galatians 4:6).
John Stott perceptively states, "He sent his Son that we
might have the *status* of sonship, and he sent his Spirit that
we might have an *experience* of it."[9]

We were once ruined, destitute children of wrath,
sons of disobedience, without Christ and without hope.
But now, because of God's great love, we belong in
his family: he is our Father, we are his children. It is no
wonder that John encourages us to marvel: "See what
kind of love the Father has given to us, that we should be
called children of God; and so we are" (1 John 3:1).

So if you are a Christian, you are not only a justified
sinner; you are a child of God by the grace of adoption.
This conveys something much more intimate than a mere
legal declaration can ever accomplish: "To be right with
God the Judge is a great thing, but to be loved and cared
for by God the Father is greater."[10] When God chose you,
when he predestined you, it was not some cold, sterile,
clinical decree. He chose to make you his child.

"Adoption as sons" ought to be the controlling
category for how we think about our relationship with
God, if only because it tells us that we have a secure relationship with the Father. In adoption, the Father, through
his Son and Spirit, assures us that we belong to him and
that he belongs to us. As a result, we can trust him, imitate
him (Ephesians 5:1), and obey him (1 Peter 1:14–19)…
even through the trials and challenges of adopting
children.

Four

THE GRACE OF ADOPTION: MINISTRY

Alex's first social worker said he had never seen a situation as bad. For the sake of Alex's birth mom, I will simply say that his life with her was dangerous and unsanitary. This little boy was in dire circumstances and had no way to rescue himself. He needed to be rescued. Without intervention from an outside source, he would have languished in his miserable condition.

Not all adoption stories begin like our son's does. Some begin with the hard but free decision of a birth mother and therefore do not require outside intervention. But all adoption stories begin with grief—the brokenness of a natural family. Therefore, all adoption is a ministry of mercy. Adoptive parents are called to step intentionally into brokenness for the purpose of healing. They make boys and girls, whose biological parents cannot raise them, into their own sons and daughters. This is mercy, and it will require a lifetime of ministry.

Rescue and Belonging

God's adoption of sinners is a profound redemptive act of rescue, and sometimes the adoption of a child is as well. God alone opens our eyes to our need of rescue from sin and death—a marvelous discovery enabled only by the Holy Spirit. We see the Son entering our world, entering our misery and affliction. We see the Son as a merciful and faithful High Priest securing our redemption in fulfillment of the Father's mission. We embrace the rescuer and his rescue. We are filled with joy at the Father's love, the Son's sacrifice, and the Spirit's call.

Just as all sinners need to be rescued from their slavery to sin, some children need to be rescued from the sin of others. Some are in an environment of death, perhaps due to drugs or alcohol or the cold institutionalizing of a human soul.[11] They cannot help themselves, and may not even realize the danger in their circumstances. They need hope and healing, and by God's grace an adoptive family can provide just those things. As Julie Smith Lowe has written, "Adoption is a mirror image of what God does for his people. Adoption redeems the broken lives of children, just as God adopts us and redeems our brokenness and sinfulness."[12] Of course, as our family's story attests, this redemption rarely happens quickly, cleanly, or easily.

Good adoptive parents pursue their children with fierce love and determination, imitating the Father's pursuit of sinners for salvation. And just as all children of God are truly "heirs according to promise" (Galatians 3:29), all children who join a family through adoption are truly members of that new family, with all the rights and privileges that would come naturally to biological children. This means, though, that every adoptive family is inherently diverse—just as God's family is quite diverse—and all the more beautiful for it. Children-by-adoption bring something new and different to their new families that is often beautiful but also challenging. When we adopted Alex, he became a true Borgman—but at the same time, we Borgmans were also changed forever. All that Alex is and all that he came from instantly became an integral part of the Borgman family story.

The simple reality of adoption is enough to make some adopted children feel a profound disconnection from their families. The biological differences between him and others in his family will probably be obvious on some level, and where there is "difference," there is opportunity for discontent. Adoption can cause emotional distress as well. Even if the most danger your child ever experienced was in utero as his mother felt the stress and shame of an unexpected pregnancy, your child may still suffer physiologically and emotionally.[13] An adoption story like that may not begin with rescue as such, but it still requires the intentional ministry work of healing and belonging. By God's grace, adoptive families can help their children experience just that.

The "What If?" Question

When Alex has been particularly challenging, Ariel and I have sometimes asked ourselves the "What if?" question—where would Alex be and what would his life look like if we had not adopted him? This has helped us express gratitude for the life he has in our family. It has also helped us reflect on the blessing that adoption has been for our family and for Alex, and given us courage for the long haul of parenting.

Once while in the Far East, I shared this hypothetical question with some adoptive parents. A mother in the group started sobbing. When she gained control she said through the interpreter, "I have never thought about that concerning my son. I have thought, 'where would I be if Jesus hadn't saved me,' but I have never thought that about him. My heart is encouraged to be patient and persevering." Parents, if you struggle because of your experience with adoption, I would encourage you to ask yourselves that same question. What if you hadn't adopted your child? You might find help by contemplating the answer.

At the same time, I do *not* recommend that you focus your adopted child on that question. In my experience, the "What if?" question is not one that adopted children naturally ask themselves. In fact, they often wonder what it would be like to live instead with their birth families,[14] and may imagine it would be better!

Especially coming from you, the "What if?" question could make them feel like a mere ministry project who "ought to be more grateful," and it could tempt you to feel like heroes. It can also make children ashamed of their natural longings for their birth families—and they should never feel shame for that love. This means that you need to handle even casual conversations about their adoption with care. Your child won't naturally overflow with wonder, love, and gratitude at having been adopted, even if life was dire prior to the adoption. Remember that every adopted child suffers a grievous loss: that of a biological mother and father. This is a rejection they may never completely understand. Only God can heal that hurt. An adoptive family has a special duty to do their best to honor and love their children's first families, even as they help their children feel like the true sons and daughters they are.

A Ministry Mindset

Adoptive parents obviously make sacrifices to bring a Christ-like ministry of mercy to their adoptive children, and they need great courage and determination to help their children feel like what they are—true members of their new families. In the face of this challenge, continually trust in your salvation and your Savior to meet all your needs. Then love your children with no demand for love or gratitude in return (see Luke 6:35–36).

Because we bear the image of God, we are made to be thankful creatures (Romans 1:21). Ingratitude is a manifestation of our depravity and rebellion against God, and all parents ought to cultivate gratitude in their children. But if you adopt and expect gratitude for it, you will probably be disappointed. Ask yourself why you pursued adoption in the first place. Did you want a pat on the back? Honor for rescuing someone from a dangerous place? The gratitude of your children? Or did you want to obey God in something you believed he had called you to do? If so, look to him for your reward. You should certainly not look for that from your children.

We must go into adoption with this kind of ministry mentality. How do you know when you have it? Simple: when you bring to this calling no expectations and a heart full of compassion. Do not demand that your children respond to your act of adoption with overflowing appreciation, emotional attachment, or even regular familial affection. Your children might feel those things, but my experience says that is the exception, not the rule. Your child at times may even cry out in anger, "Why did you adopt me? I wish you had never adopted me!" In times like that, you can take comfort in the knowledge that you have obeyed God in expanding your family through adoption. Your heavenly Father rescued you from the domain of darkness and placed you in his Son's kingdom (Colossians 1:13). You can therefore trust him for whatever final rescue he may accomplish for your children.

Five
THE GRIT OF ADOPTION: WARFARE

Ariel would greet me with exasperation in her voice. "I am glad you are home. Can you deal with him?"

"What's the problem?"

Did I really have to ask? The answers could range from, "I have asked Alex to take the garbage out four times and he sits there ignoring me," to "Alex told me he didn't have any homework. Now, at 10 pm, he tells me he needs me to take him to Walmart to buy something for a project due in the morning. I told him he couldn't do that to me. Then he said I didn't care if he flunked his class."

The examples could go on, but you get the point.

Adoption presented me with a special challenge. I was raised to never ignore or disrespect my parents; they did not tolerate such behavior. So Alex's attitude created a problem I did not know how to deal with. He seemed to have a special talent for ignoring and disrespecting us, and he could do those things for a long time, regardless of the consequences. This tested my patience. It also revealed that I had made an idol out of being respected (more on idolatry in the next chapter).

It took me a while to recognize that the real problem wasn't Alex at all. The problem was the Enemy of our souls.

Fight the Real Enemy

For many years, coming home from work felt like walking into a war zone. This was not the case *every single day*, just most days. The tension was thick. Ariel would be either withdrawn or angry. Alex would be irritated and easily angered. Any word of correction was met with defiance. Any word of direction was ignored. Disrespect flowed easily from his heart and mouth, and anger and harsh words flowed readily from mine. It seemed we were at war. If bombs weren't flying, we were usually under cold war conditions.

In fact, adoption *is* war, but adoptive parents must remember that, despite how it sometimes feels, this war is never with the child. Adoption is a war "against the rulers, against the authorities, against the cosmic powers over this present darkness, against the spiritual forces of evil in the heavenly places" (Ephesians 6:12). Satan opposes our mission, parents. He would much rather have children live in abusive and negligent homes or in orphanages — anonymous, unwanted, and largely ignored. And the last thing the Enemy wants to risk is to have children raised in the love and light of Christ's gospel.

All parenting is spiritual warfare. In fact, the whole

Christian life is spiritual warfare.[15] But some children come from dark places, and parenting them means that you will fight a particular battle for their hearts and minds. So take up the whole armor of God and remember that the victory is his. This kind of "remembering" is what I call a biblically wise gospel orientation—that is, a mindset informed by the whole counsel of God and focused on the gospel. You need to keep this perspective if you have any hope of parenting an adopted child well—and the only way to keep this perspective is to wage war.

Let yourself get entangled in whatever real or perceived misery you might experience because you adopted, and you can lose perspective. There is much at stake here. Self-pity and resentment toward your child for your present challenges will turn you inward—the quickest way to lose ground in your battle.

You need God's wisdom if you are going to maintain the proper perspective. A biblically wise gospel orientation keeps you looking past self-pity, personal insults, and inconvenience, and helps you maintain a warfare mentality. It drives you to "be strong in the Lord and in the strength of his might" (Ephesians 6:10). Such dependence on God's strength and appropriation of God's provision also helps you to guard your own heart.[16]

Persevere with Grace

Remember that parenting is both ministry and spiritual battle. All these struggles, challenges, and conflicts go beyond flesh and blood. Just as regarding parenting as ministry keeps your heart compassionate, the reality of spiritual warfare keeps you dependent on the Lord and alert to the schemes of the devil. Satan does not believe in the sanctity of life, the sanctity of marriage, or the beauty of the family. He will use your adoptive struggles to wage war on your marriage, on your family, and on your faith. He is a murderer and the father of lies (John 8:44).

I remember a particular time when Ariel and I did not respond well after one of Alex's angry eruptions. Not only were we angry with him for his disrespectful and disruptive behavior, but there was a growing tension between the two of us. Ariel told me how angry and hurt she was, and then I said it.

"This is your fault. You wanted to adopt him. If you had only listened to me! I told you he would bring turmoil into our family."

I still can't believe I said it.

The words hurt her so badly. It was obvious as soon as I spoke. But they could not be taken back. My flesh was at work—my selfish, sinful, wicked heart. But Satan was also at work. We had given him a foothold and he was on the attack. After a while, we realized what was happening. I asked for forgiveness. We reconciled and prayed. I knew I had lost my warfare mentality, and it had cost us.

God has graciously provided us his armor so that we can stand firm (Ephesians 6:14–17). This should shape our prayers and inform our perspective in the daily grind of life. This applies to all of life, but it must also apply to our adoptive challenges and struggles. We cannot afford to be ignorant of Satan's schemes (2 Corinthians 2:11). So the next time "all hell seems to be breaking loose," take a moment to remind yourself of the warfare and call in reinforcements from the captain of your salvation (whom Hebrews 2:10 tells us will bring many sons to glory). Ask for the right perspective, and then move ahead in the grace, wisdom, and power of God's Spirit.

Six
GRACE TO GUARD OUR HEARTS

A few years ago, some young married couples in our church were watching Paul Tripp's video series, "What Did You Expect?" One week they invited my wife and me to come share our "vast" wisdom with them. We watched, listened, took notes, and then offered some thoughts. We made sure to remind the younger couples that while the series is about marriage, it is more importantly about our hearts.

On the drive home, Ariel and I talked about how much we had enjoyed being with the group. But we also talked about how convicting the conversation had been for us — we both admitted that we had been thinking more about how we respond to Alex than we were thinking about our marriage.

During the video, Tripp took an open water bottle and shook it until the water started coming out. He said our hearts are just like that when we are shaken — what's inside begins coming out. That illustration hit both of us, and we prayed about it together in the car.

Adoption, like marriage and parenting in general, has
a way of ruthlessly exposing what is in our hearts. It is a
great opportunity for ministry, as we have seen, but that
means it is also a great revealer of idols and sinful attitudes.
Ariel and I began to see that our frustrations and anger
with Alex resulted from idolatry in our hearts.

> I am deeply persuaded that our idols have caused us
> to see opportunity as trial and caused us to strike back
> at our [children] with bitter words of judgment, accu-
> sation, and condemnation, behaving toward them
> with intolerance and anger. While God is calling us
> to love, accept, forgive, and serve, we are often barely
> able to be nice.[17]

I have come to the painful conviction that if we are to
receive the help we need in difficult adoptive situations,
we must diligently guard our hearts *and* be willing to
honestly examine our hearts.

Solomon reminds us, "Keep your heart with all
vigilance, for from it flow the springs of life" (Proverbs
4:23). Before we can try to help our children, we must first
understand what is going on in our own hearts. God in his
grace has put that child in your family. You will often find,
then, that God is using that child to expose idols in your
heart. Adoption is both ministry and spiritual warfare, but
it is also a very effective tool in heart surgery, idol exposure,
and (hopefully) idol destruction. We must be open to this
painful process. There is no way to move ahead and make
progress if you are holding on to idols in your own heart.

Sometimes I feel like a patient on a gurney, wearing a gown, ready to be rolled into an operating room. The only thing missing is the anesthesia, for God is not in the habit of anesthetizing us before he opens us up. When he performs "idolectomies," he does so with love and mercy, yet divine love and mercy are sometimes accompanied necessarily by pain. So as you continue reading this chapter, I hope you will be open to what the Great Physician will do. I hope you will be open to seeing idols in your heart that may hinder you in ministering to your children.

Idol: A Romanticized View of Adoption

We must guard our hearts against a romanticized view of adoption. We can see pictures, hear stories, and read books that make us think that once that child becomes a part of our home, he or she will soak up our love like a dry sponge. Maybe your child came from dangerous circumstances, and maybe he even *wanted* to be rescued. This does not necessarily mean he will blossom once he is in the safety and comfort of your home. In fact, he may become cold and distant, or defiant and angry.

You want a loving family, but what if you don't get that?

Adoptive parents want their children to experience love and belonging. They want their children to flourish. In fact, they have intentionally sought out non-biological children to love and cherish. But how you react when your dream of a loving family doesn't come true in exactly the way you had hoped will tell you where you have misplaced worship—where you have raised good desires to the level of demands.[18] Perhaps you have made an idol of rescue, which is easy to do. Prospective adoptive parents need to realize that adoption is a ministry predicated on mercy, not the happiness of the family. Our dreams may therefore be idols. And when those idols are knocked over, we can begin to lose sight of the ministry opportunities in front of us.

Sherrie Eldridge notes, "I believe that one of the most sacrificial acts of love adoptive parents can do is give up their preconceptions and agendas about what their child's views 'should' be and be open to hear the conflicting emotions and thoughts their child often experiences."[19] Expectations, agendas, and dreams of adoptive life can be nothing more than fantasy. They can prevent us from being open, tender, and compassionate. Unmet expectations can lead to huge frustration and irritability as we take the child's discontentment or disobedience as personal insult. This idol of adoption will not only damage our own hearts but also those of the children we bring into our families through adoption.[20]

Idol: The Perfect Family

We must also guard our hearts against the idol of the perfect family. In my circles, the picture of the perfect family is often propagated through ministries that advocate patriarchy, homeschooling, no college for daughters, homegrown vegetables, and baking your own bread. White Victorian families grace the covers of the books.

My wife and I fit that model in some ways: we homeschooled our kids until they got to high school, and a woman in our church used to give us homemade bread every other week. Although there is much good that comes from these types of ministries, there can also be much harm. We must use discernment. Oftentimes the proponents of this lifestyle don't recognize some of the unique customs and cultures of the biblical era. We must ask ourselves, how much of this teaching is based on the wishful thinking that a bygone era was a better time to live, and how much is actually biblical?

One Lord's Day after morning worship a man came up to me, deeply distressed. He said, "Pastor, I have a serious question for you. I look at some of the families in our church, and they don't homeschool, they let their kids go to movies, they eat fast food, they don't have nearly as many rules as we do, and they are happy! I look at my family, and I know that *we try to do everything right*. We do it by the book. We eat right, we take vitamins, we homeschool, we have family devotions twice a day, we read the right books—we should be the perfect family. But we are miserable!"

After a long discussion about the bondage of legalism, we got around to the idol of the perfect family. There is no perfect family. Families are always messy. *Always*—for families are made up only of sinners. Jay Adams reminded us years ago, "The first and most important fact to remember about a truly Christian home is that *sinners live there*."[21] I wholeheartedly believe that if homeschooling or eating a certain way or not owning a TV is your conviction, then you should follow that conviction. However, we cannot think that by doing these things we will produce something spiritual, let alone achieve the blissful happy family.[22]

When you have set up the idol of the perfect family in the high place of your heart, you will not only be disappointed with the lack of perfection, you will also see anyone who brings in problems as an enemy. You can actually put your ideal of the family above the good of your family members! If you have this attitude and then adopt, you're in for a very rough time. The idol of the perfect family is always law-driven, with little room for grace or mercy, yet adoption requires a great deal of grace *and* mercy. Where the idol of the perfect family reigns, mistakes and sins are taken as personal insults and treated like blemishes on the family name. What is ultimately at stake in such a family is not the health of the family itself, but your pride.

Ask yourself, "How do I respond to my child's inappropriate behavior, especially in public?"

- If you are more concerned about how the behavior reflects on your parenting abilities, your authority, or your godliness, you are serving an idol.
- If you suffer embarrassment because of inappropriate behavior—and your embarrassment is the biggest problem to you—you are serving an idol.
- If you take inappropriate behavior as a personal offense, you are serving an idol.
- If you are constantly asking, "Don't you know how that makes me feel?" you are serving an idol.

- If you say, "How dare you act that way after all I've done for you?" you are serving an idol.
- If you ask, "Why can't you act more like _____?" you are serving an idol.
- If you say, "Do you know how that made our family look?" you are likely serving an idol.[23]

Your response to imperfection in your children may reveal the idol of the perfect family. Do not allow that idol to stand. It will circumvent redemptive parenting, obscure grace, and eclipse the gospel. So if you are considering adoption, please ask yourself if this is indeed an idol in your heart. If it is, please do not adopt until this high place has been torn down. If you have already adopted and view your child as "the troubler," imagining that you would be a truly happy family if only this child would obey, please recognize your idol for what it is and repent of your pride and idolatry. Repent to the Lord *and* to your family. There is forgiveness and power for change in the gospel.

Idol: Domestic Peace and Quiet

We must also guard against the related idol of domestic peace and quiet. A man's home is his castle, and castles should be quiet and peaceful fortifications from the clamor of the world...right?

I have heard speakers talk about a man's home being a refuge where he can be surrounded by a loving wife, winsome children, and dogs who bring slippers and entertain the family (okay, the dog part is an exaggeration). Is that what home should be?

This one is a serious battle for me. As a pastor, I spend most of my day studying and the rest counseling. If I have two or three counseling sessions in a day, I really want to come home to peace. Helping others in turmoil makes me long for that. *All* I want when I come home after a long day is enough peace and quiet to sip on a Snapple and watch the Giants game.

But as I've described, I have so many times come home to my supposed castle and found it was actually a war zone! The war looked the same for years, with Alex at the center of the battle: Alex disrespectful, Alex disobedient, Alex starting verbal firestorms with everyone in the house, and Ariel at her wit's end. This was essentially our "normal." Ariel wouldn't want to burden me with these daily issues, but she also needed resolution and deliverance from her no-win situation.

What would typically happen? Usually I had an immediate confrontation with Alex. His attitude and behavior had to be addressed; that was legitimate. But there was almost always something else at work in me — an irritability driven by underlying questions like, "Why is he doing this to me? Doesn't he know I just want to come home to peace?"

Honestly, I took the lack of peace personally and rarely reacted well. I don't want to excuse Alex's inconsiderate or disrespectful behavior, but I often felt resentful simply because he was keeping me from my idol. Instead of recognizing an opportunity for working the gospel into Alex's heart, as well as mine and Ariel's, all I could see was yet another inconvenience.

If peace and quiet is my idol, I assume these things are mine by rights. Anyone who stands in the way of this idol is therefore my enemy. I have lost count of how many times I have made Alex my enemy simply because he threatened my idol.

In these moments, what was actually happening? Alex's behavior was displaying sin in his heart, and revealing slightly less obvious sin in my heart. One thing I wish I had reminded myself of more often in those moments is this: before I could ever help Alex, I needed to see that my sinful responses grew out of the fact that I was valuing my own peace and quiet above what was best for our son. I was exalting my leisure above his deep need.

When Ariel was worn out with Alex, I had the opportunity to minister to her as well. In these moments, it was me whom God was calling to bring grace and wisdom to the situation. But as long as I harbored the idol of peace and quiet in my heart, I was useless. Peace is good, but it is not my birthright. Peace with God has been secured for me through Jesus' justifying grace (Romans 5:1), and I must seek and work for peace with others (Romans 12:18, 14:19).

Keep Yourselves from Idols

John Calvin famously said that our hearts are idol factories.[24] Idols can powerfully cloud our perspectives on both ministry and warfare. As adoptive parents, therefore, our first step in effective parenting amidst the challenges must be to face our own carefully manufactured idols. There is grace in recognizing our idols and identifying the

67

underlying heart issues. But we also need grace to repent and guard our hearts. After all, the apostle John ends his first epistle with these words: "Little children, keep yourselves from idols" (1 John 5:21).

Maybe you have seen in this chapter an idol or two that, when threatened, you've been willing to go to war over. Thank God for showing you that—but understand that he has shown you so he can help you deal with it. Go to the cross for forgiveness and seek help from the one who promises to help us by giving us grace and mercy in our time of need (Hebrews 4:16).

Seven
GRACE TO READJUST OUR THINKING

From the time our daughter was an infant, Ariel and I wanted to be biblical in our childrearing. Being responsible for a little human being made in the image and likeness of God weighed on us, and we took it very seriously. We read good books about biblical parenting. We listened to hours of lessons by a pastor who taught us how to not foul up our children.

My wife and I got the principles down. We knew the verses and took them to heart, "Folly is bound up in the heart of a child, but the rod of discipline drives it far from him" (Proverbs 22:15). We knew the whys and hows of biblical discipline, and I taught them with great vigor to our congregation.

By the way, if you have a compliant first child, it is not because you are awesome parents who have mastered parenthood. It is because God was merciful.

Because then came Alex. I am not saying Alex required

us to abandon biblical principles, but he made us reconsider how we applied them. Alex challenged our confidence and showed us that our methods were not "one size fits all." At times we have been shaken to our parental core, wondering if we really knew what we were doing at all.

Paul Tripp brought relief to my troubled heart when I read these words, "Your struggles with your adopted child will not always be the result of your mistakes. Sometimes your struggles will stem from inherent differences in the hardwiring of your child. *Those differences will require different parenting strategies from the ones you use with your natural children.*"[25] I was freed then to think outside my fairly narrow box and reconsider how certain truths applied to Alex. The need to think differently had been brought home to me in painful ways.

Parenting is hard work that requires real effort. James Dobson reminded us of this years ago with the title of his book, *Parenting is Not for Cowards*. We frequently parent by default, losing focus on biblical truths and heart issues. Many of us have struggled with being consistently inconsistent. However, to actually rethink strategies — to question the efficacy of long-held methods and then do something differently — requires fresh grace from God. To position ourselves to receive that grace, let's begin with some key truths about our children.

Key Truths about Our Children

There are three factors we must keep in mind about adopted children: they bear God's image, they are fallen, and adoption affects them.

Image-bearers. Our children are made in the image and likeness of God (Genesis 1:26–28). Because they are image-bearers, they have dignity as human beings. They are fearfully and wonderfully made (Psalm 139:13–16). They were made to image God throughout this world. They were made for a relationship with God in this world. They were also made as creatures with a never-dying soul. This key truth, that our children are image-bearers, requires us to treat them with dignity and respect.

Fallen. Yet our children are not only image-bearers, they are fallen image-bearers. They not only have dignity, they suffer from depravity. Our children come into this world as sinners in Adam (Romans 5:12) and have fallen natures (Jeremiah 17:9). Our children sin because they are sinners. They have a natural bent to sin and rebellion (Psalm 58:3, Romans 3:10–18). We don't have to give them lessons on how to be selfish with their toys or how to lie to avoid getting into trouble. These sins, and many more, come naturally.

Apart from the regeneration of the Holy Spirit, our children's minds are set on the flesh (Romans 8:5–8). They have an agenda, which is to follow their own desires and to please themselves. This applies to every child born into this world, whether the offspring of believers or unbelievers. Our children are thus a paradox in that they have dignity as human beings yet are also depraved. The capacity for great things and for great sin dwells within those little hearts.

Affected by adoption. There is also an "X factor" with our adopted children, something that is certain to be present yet not entirely predictable—adoption will affect every adopted child, in one way or another and to one degree or another. I am amazed at how many adoptive parents deny this. The fact that the mother who bore them is not the one raising them will affect even those children brought into an adoptive home immediately after birth. If you're inclined to disagree on that point, please be open-minded through the remainder of this section.

These three key truths—image-bearers, fallen, and affected by adoption— give us the necessary starting point to be an agent of grace in our children's lives. While we can relate to the first two truths (since we ourselves are fallen image-bearers), the third requires us to work hard at identifying and adopting new strategies. In particular, we must try to think like our adopted children think. This is much more difficult than it sounds, and at times it will seem impossible. To do it effectively, we need God's help and wisdom.

Thinking Like They Think

Jesus teaches us in the Golden Rule, "So whatever you wish that others would do to you, do also to them, for this is the Law and the Prophets" (Matthew 7:12). One thing we all want is to be understood, in matters both big and small. To feel misunderstood can be extremely frustrating. This is true for all of us: infants who can't even speak, children and adolescents who may withdraw and turn sullen rather than try to explain themselves, and adults who sometimes won't explain if they think their hearers just wouldn't understand. Obviously, then, being misunderstood can be as much of a challenge for adopted children as it can for anyone else. Adoptive parents committed to loving these children dare not assume otherwise.

So where do we begin in this quest of trying to understand our adoptive children? In other words, how do we begin to think like they think?

Rosaria Butterfield has written some of the most important words on adoption I have ever read, and they give us a good starting point for trying to understand our children.

> No child asks to be adopted. No child asks for incompetent or rejecting birth parents. No child wants to be told how "lucky" he is to be adopted. Adoption always starts with a loss. Adoption always combines ambiguous loss with unrequested gain. An adopted child faces this paradox—this ambiguous grief—at each developmental stage. His or her family must choose to either welcome the complexity or make the child go it alone. We choose to walk alongside our children, even as we don't always understand how deep or how raw the complexity rests. The journey is frightful. At its core is this: do I love Jesus enough to face my children's potential rejection of me?[26]

As a rule, our adopted children will always know they are different. They will typically look different, and if we have biological children, our adopted children will often insist they are treated differently. Sometimes they are.

I know an adoptive mother who decided not to tell her children they were adopted because she "wanted them to feel 'normal.'" But they always knew something was different, always knew they didn't look like each other, or like mom or dad. Then one day they were snooping around and found the adoption papers. Embarrassed, they couldn't mention it. As the children were approaching 18, the mom finally told them. Imagine the regret that unfolded in her heart when she learned they had known for years.

Sherrie Eldridge notes,

> The majority of adoptees do run into ambivalent or painful feelings about adoption at some point in their lives. Psychologists call the thoughts and feelings many adoptees experience "cognitive dissonance": adoption experts call it "genealogical bewilderment." The true experts—adoptees themselves—put it in much more earthly terms:

- "It's a vague feeling inside that something is wrong."
- "It feels like a part of me is missing."
- "It's an intangible battle between heart and soul."
- "I have spent my whole life roaming and never felt stable."
- "I search for answers I am never sure I can find."
- "I look at life through a lens of rejection, expecting it at every turn."[27]

We are all interpreters and we are all social beings. As

Paul Tripp reminds us,

> People are meaning-makers; we have been created
> with the marvelous ability to think. We are always
> organizing, interpreting, and explaining what is going
> on inside us and around us.…We do not live life based
> on the bare facts of our existence; we live our lives
> according to our *interpretation* of those facts.[28]

Adoption complicates these aspects of the child's
life. She not only has to interpret life like everyone else,
she also has an added filter on the lens. She not only has
to navigate through the social relationships of life like
everyone else, she has to navigate with a compass broken
by rejection. God's grace compels us to "Put on then, as
God's chosen ones, holy and beloved, compassionate
hearts, kindness, humility, meekness, and patience, bearing
with one another" (Colossians 3:12–13). That heart of
compassion should drive us to view every situation
bearing on the lives of our adopted children through the
interpretive grid and social compass that *they* possess.

This means we must stop and take the time to ask
ourselves questions like these about our adopted children.

- *How does she think about this?*
- *How does he interpret what just happened?*
- *How does he think he should act right now?*
- *Why* isn't *she thinking about how she should act right now?*
  If we don't ask such questions of ourselves, we may

be trampling over our children's thoughts and emotions, failing to do to them what we want others to do to us — to understand us.

This will take patience on our part. It is so easy, especially for fathers, to jump to correction mode and try to fix what seems to be broken. It is hard for us to take a minute to ask ourselves, *How are they seeing this situation? Why are they acting this way? What is behind it?*

So there the little guy is, surrounded by birthday presents, donning a birthday hat — and looking melancholy. All his friends are playing and having fun, but he is sitting there quietly.

Dad enthusiastically says, "Go play with your friends. This is your day!" He gets up and mopes toward his friends. Dad, a little irritated, then says, "Hey, wait a minute. Look at all that we've done for you. Look, your friends are all here for you. What's wrong with you? Why are you so ungrateful?"

Putting on a heart of compassion prevents us from rushing to assume the problem is ingratitude. A heart of compassion will ask, "Why is he so quiet? What's on his mind?" Maybe he is wondering if his birth-mom is thinking of him on his birthday. Maybe he is wondering if she even remembers. We will never know if we fail to think like he thinks or fail to ask good heart-to-heart questions.

We were confronted with our failure to do this early on with Alex. We would tell him, "Alex, go put your toys away, put on your pajamas, brush your teeth, and come out for family worship." As the other two children sat in the living room waiting for us to start, Ariel or I would get up to see what Alex was doing. On more than one occasion we discovered him standing on his little stool in front of the bathroom mirror and splashing the mirror by flicking the bristles on his toothbrush. We would reprimand him for his "disobedience." Sometimes he would be spanked.

We then attended a seminar on Fetal Alcohol Syndrome. We learned that alcohol is a solvent that goes through the mother's bloodstream right to the baby. This causes developmental delays in the frontal lobe of the child's brain. We also learned that such delays have a direct impact on the child's ability to sequence. A child with FAS needs to be given one directive or command at a time. If there are too many, the child can become confused and easily distracted. The seminar speaker then gave the example of "clean your room, put on your pajamas, and brush your teeth." Our hearts sank as we realized we had disciplined Alex for something over which he had little to no control. That knowledge altered our parenting strategy. It helped us to try to be understanding and to think like he thinks.

Our adopted children have thoughts that would never occur to us. This is why we need to give them a safe environment to talk about what they think and how they feel. Eldridge again notes, "The thing adoptees need most is the freedom to express their conflicting emotions without fear of judgment…Adoptees need a safe place to share their feelings about adoption, both positive and negative, and to feel protected and loved unconditionally regardless of what comes out of their mouths."[29]

One night when Alex was about 12, he was being particularly irritating to everyone, just a walking button-pusher. As was often the case, he began focusing all his energies on his mother. Ariel responded sharply to one of his jabs and things escalated quickly. Alex became immediately disrespectful. I intervened with wisdom and grace….I wish! I intervened by sending Alex to his room. I went back to my reading or baseball game, only to realize that an hour had passed since I heard anything out of Alex. That nearly always spells trouble, so I got up to investigate.

I walked into Alex's room to find him and Ariel sitting on the floor, crying. Alex has never been the crying type, so I asked the insightful question, "Is everything all right?" At Ariel's urging, Alex then said tearfully, "I asked mom why my birth mom didn't want me." My heart broke as I realized that for most of Alex's life he'd had an agony tucked away deep in his heart, an awful sense of loss and rejection. *Was I not good enough? Was I not loved enough? Why would someone give away their child?* These questions must have haunted him daily, inevitably distorting his view of life and relationships.

I decided to explain to Alex the circumstances sur-rounding his adoption. I talked about why he had needed to be in foster care. We spoke openly but not disparag-ingly of his birth mom's addictions. We spoke about our attempts to help her and our love for him. I also told him frankly about my reluctance to adopt and how his mom had championed his cause because of her deep love for and commitment to him. We helped him put his loss in the context of a birth mom who loved him but was simply unable to care for him. We also spoke directly about how drugs and alcohol can ruin people's lives and cause them to make bad moral decisions that hurt other people. We talked about how he has been God's gift to us and how we hope that he feels we are a gift from God to him.

As this lengthy and tearful discussion was unfolding, I had an epiphany of sorts.

"Alex, I know you and your mom have always butted heads and struggled with each other. Do you know why?"

Alex responded with a revelation of his own. "I thought that mom might not want me either."

As you might imagine, the waterworks got turned on all the way now. We all sat there crying with each other. Ariel held Alex.

This didn't excuse any of Alex's sinful behavior over the years, but suddenly things started to make more sense. Alex had been protecting himself. It was easier for him to keep Ariel at arm's length, testing her, seeing when she would finally give up. He almost expected it. If, like his birth mother, she was "not going to want him either," why should he open up? Although the thinking was flawed, immature, and misguided, it was the way he interpreted life, and especially his relationship with his mom. Had we picked up on this sooner, we could have more intentionally affirmed our love for Alex and our commitment to him. Instead, we saw everything as rebellion or defiance—and nothing more—and disciplined accordingly.

We cannot begin to know everything our adopted

children think. We probably can't even fully grasp their interpretive grids. But inside those hearts are not simply sinners who sin, but human beings who have suffered a trauma that has warped their thinking, their emotions, and sometimes their brains. We will not be effective agents of grace until we try to understand them and seek to learn to think like they think — or at least ask good questions so we can gain some insight. That night with Alex brought a breakthrough that radically altered our understanding of him, especially with respect to the doubt, struggles, pain, and confusion that accompanied his many acts of defiance.

Rethinking parental strategies will require us to humble ourselves before God and before our children. Confessing to our adopted children that we have made bad decisions and mistakes — thus admitting we don't have all the answers — takes humility. That may sound like a cliché to you, but many Christian parents often do act like they know all the answers. We do *not* automatically understand these children God puts into our homes. It takes time, grace, and compassion. It demands that we do our best to understand them and try to think like they think.

Eight
GRACE TO AVOID PROVOCATION

When I was a teenager, our youth pastor broke open an egg and dumped it on the table. "Can you put it back?" he asked.

Being teenagers, we thought we would be smart, say yes, and give it a try. Of course, we just made a huge mess, but the lesson took: the broken egg is like our words. Once they come out of our mouths we can never put them back.

I haven't forgotten that lesson. I only wish I had practiced it more often over the years.

Of all the parenting mistakes I have made, especially with Alex, I regret my hurtful words the most. Words spoken in frustration and anger have wounded my son. The Bible teaches us — and experience backs it up — that words are incredibly powerful. "Death and life are in the power of the tongue, and those who love it will eat its fruits" (Proverbs 18:21). The Bible also teaches us that our words come from our hearts (Matthew 12:37), and can even have a kind of lethal power: "There is one whose rash words are like sword thrusts" (Proverbs 12:18a).

But no one surpasses James in describing the destructive power of our words.

> So also the tongue is a small member, yet it boasts of great things. How great a forest is set ablaze by such a small fire! And the tongue is a fire, a world of unrighteousness. The tongue is set among our members, staining the whole body, setting on fire the entire course of life, and set on fire by hell (James 3:5–6).

I will never forget one occasion at a pastors' conference. I was exchanging good-natured banter with a friend when he stopped and said, "You know, you hurt my feelings once." I was on a roll, so I retorted, "Impossible! You don't have any feelings." I could see my words wounded him, so I apologized. Later that evening this big, strong, assertive man broke down and told me that growing up all he heard from his dad was criticism and name-calling. His father told him repeatedly that he was no good and would never amount to anything. My friend went on, "Even to this day, certain words can fill me with a sense of shame all over again." That was one moment when I wished, too late, that I had remembered the egg lesson.

Although I have never intentionally sought to hurt Alex with my words, I have said things for which I am ashamed. I have asked his forgiveness, yet I live with the reality that he will always remember those words and the hurt they have caused. It sobers me to think he will probably remember more clearly the harsh words I have said than he will my affirming words of love and encouragement. That's not his fault, it's mine. Contrary to the old adage, words can and do hurt us. Even as I write this, my heart is filled with sorrow over my sins of the tongue and the imprints they have made on my son.

But our words can also be used for affirmation and edification, conduits for God's grace, for "the tongue of the wise brings healing" (Proverbs 12:18b). Paul gives us a one of the most comprehensive statements on our words: "Let no corrupting talk come out of your mouths, but only such as is good for building up, as fits the occasion, that it may give grace to those who hear" (Ephesians 4:29). Our words are never just words.

I am ashamed to admit I have said things to Alex I would never say to my biological children. I could point to the fact that Alex pushes my buttons in ways my other children do not, but that does not justify my harsh words—nothing can come out of my mouth that isn't already in my heart.

When we forget who our real Enemy is (Ephesians 6:12), or when we give place to certain idols, our child can become an object of our anger. Hurtful words may then be close behind. I have had to work diligently on this, and I have learned these lessons far more out of failure than success. I trust that such lessons will lead us to Christ for forgiveness and, through his Spirit, transformation.

Put a Guard over Your Mouth

A soft answer turns away wrath, but a harsh word stirs up anger (Proverbs 15:1).

Set a guard, O LORD, over my mouth; keep watch over the door of my lips! (Psalm 141:3).

Know this, my beloved brothers: let every person be quick to hear, slow to speak, slow to anger. (James 1:19).

It can't be overemphasized how important our words are. If they are life or death, if they can edify or corrupt, if they can turn away wrath or stir up anger, then we must ask God for the grace to keep a guard over our mouths and be slow to speak. This is true in all of life, but it is especially important to be wise about our words when dealing with our adopted children.

As I mentioned earlier, our adopted children operate from a framework that we simply may not understand. Some claim that these children act out of anger. Others say they act out of fear. Either way, they are protecting themselves, and as adoptive parents we must understand that *there may be words and tones that trigger in them the need to protect themselves*. Please hear that.

Instead of making our children feel safe, words that are harsh or unwise may make them feel threatened. A particular tone of voice may put them on the defensive. Nagging can tempt them to anger or even violence. At every moment we need to do our best, by God's grace, to make our words edifying and reaffirming. Even in correction or confrontation, we need to guard the heart and watch the mouth. We need to excel at "speaking the truth in love" (Ephesians 4:15).

If we are trying to think like they think, we also need to hear as they hear. If our children are constantly reacting negatively to our correction, we should think about how that correction is proceeding from our mouths. Not every word of correction is *spoken* correctly. They will probably hear *how* we speak before they hear *what* we say.

Avoid the Escalation

Years ago I went on a ride-along with a sheriff's deputy. As I asked him about stressful situations in his job, he told me, "When I need assistance or backup, I always know there are certain officers who will come in and help me defuse the situation. But I also know if certain other officers show up on the scene, I will end up in a fight. They don't have a clue how to defuse a situation; they only know how to escalate one."

Perhaps we parents are sometimes like that second group of officers. We arrive on the scene to enforce the law and impose our will. But do we have the ability to defuse a tense situation, and not just escalate it?

The apostle Paul warned, "Fathers, do not provoke your children to anger" (Ephesians 6:4). He also exhorted, "Fathers, do not provoke your children, lest they become discouraged" (Colossians 3:21). We must not believe the myth that the parent is always right — Paul certainly didn't believe it! Parents can sin against their children by "goading them to resentment," as the New English Bible translates this phrase. Parents certainly can irritate and embitter their children so they become discouraged. We need to be honest enough with ourselves to ask, *What am*

I doing to provoke him? What am I doing that exasperates her? What am I doing that escalates these situations? We should also be bold enough to ask our children similar questions. "Tell me what I do that provokes you."

Lou Priolo gives us a list of 25 ways parents provoke their children to anger.[30] I'll just list 10 of them here, but I encourage you to get the book and dig into all of them. Priolo cites relevant Scripture as he discusses each point, so the book is a good study for all parents who want to communicate better with their children. For now, you might easily imagine how behaviors like these could provoke children to anger:

1. Habitually disciplining while angry
2. Being inconsistent with discipline
3. Having double standards
4. Being legalistic
5. Constantly finding fault
6. Not listening to your child's opinion or taking his or her "side of the story" seriously
7. Comparing them to others
8. Failing to keep your promises
9. Unrealistic expectations
10. Practicing favoritism

What a list—plus there are 15 more and I'm guilty on most counts! When we engage in these kinds of actions, we unnecessarily escalate conflict with our children. This is obviously true when it comes to our biological children, but it may be acutely true with an adopted child, for the reasons I have been explaining: we may be triggering responses in the hearts of our children that we don't understand, and they don't either.

Avoiding escalation with Alex was a painful but important lesson for Ariel and me. One thing we found especially challenging after a while was the monotonous predictability of his behavior. It didn't take too long before we could virtually write the script to each conflict before it happened.

1. We would correct Alex for something, often guilty of many of the things mentioned in Priolo's list.
2. He would snap back at us.
3. We would reprimand him for disrespect.
4. He would retort with some cutting remark.
5. We would try to explain to him why he was wrong.
6. He would dig in, no matter how illogical or irrational his position.

From there, things nearly always got worse. If his older brother and friends were there telling him he was wrong and needed to obey, Alex would just conclude there was an evil conspiracy at work. Despite the amazing predictability of this pattern, we fell right into it more times than I could have ever thought possible. In the early stages of these conflicts, when the situation was still essentially in our control, we nevertheless allowed it to escalate until Alex became provoked. At that point things usually turned ugly and frequently got *out* of our control.

A similar pattern tended to unfold whenever we

tried to discipline Alex. Because of my convictions on parental authority and the fifth commandment, for years I was unwilling to budge or compromise. When Alex was younger, of course, it was a simple matter of me being stronger than him. But by the time he was 12 or 13, brute force was no longer an option.

To my shame, it never occurred to me simply to ask if there was something more going on here than just a disobedient son. Were *we* doing anything that was adding fuel to the fire—or even starting a fire?

Remember the words of Paul Tripp, "Those differences [in your adopted child] will require different parenting strategies from the ones you use with your natural children."[31] I wanted to start doing things differently, but Ariel thought that would be compromise. By that point, however, I was pretty sure that our methods of discipline were not only ineffective, but impractical. I didn't yet see the problem clearly, but I did see that our current solution was really no solution at all.

In a discipline situation, Alex would not respond to privileges lost or rewards offered. By the time he was 12, spanking had been off the table for a while. As I tried to be more calm and reasonable with him—looking for some approach that might work—Ariel said I was being too lenient. She thought I was letting him get away with things we never let our other kids get away with. In a sense, she was right. With our other children I was able to use biblical approaches that helped. With Alex, it often seemed that nothing helped. By this time he was old enough to drive, and the tension was growing between

Ariel and me over this matter. I knew we needed advice, and I certainly didn't want to see this apparent impasse give Satan yet another foothold in our family. So we went to dinner with some dear, wise friends to discuss it, and to my relief they agreed we should look for a way to decrease the confrontations.

We soon had just such an opportunity. Ariel asked Alex to do something, but he ignored her. Ariel looked to me to intervene. I said, "Alex, your Mom has made a reasonable request. Ignoring her is disrespectful. Please do what she asked." Alex looked at me with defiance. He walked over to the table, grabbed his keys, and said, "I'm leaving." I knew from Ariel's expression that she wanted me to stop him. All I said was, "Alex, it is wrong for you to leave." He kept walking. We heard him start the car and drive away.

Ariel was in disbelief. "Why did you let him just leave?"

I responded, "What did you want me to do? I am not going to escalate things by trying to take his keys or driver's license or by sending him to his room."

Ariel gave in.

About 15 minutes later, her phone rang. It was Alex.

"Mom, please forgive me for ignoring you and not doing what you asked me to do. I was wrong. I was also wrong for leaving. I'm sorry."

He then asked to speak to me. "Dad, I was wrong for leaving and not doing what I was asked to do. Please forgive me."

Alex came home and apologized again. He did what

he was told. He seemed rather subdued the rest of the
night. An hour or so after the incident, I asked him what
had happened when he left.

He said, "I went and parked. I thought about what I
did and knew it was wrong."

Later, Ariel and I made some observations about the
incident. First, when correcting or confronting Alex, we
have often done so in a way that immediately provokes
him. Second, Alex almost never apologizes—especially
when he is confronted and knows he simply needs to
admit he is wrong. Third, if I had tried to force him to stay
or obey, the situation would certainly have intensified—
we would have both ended up angry, and Alex would still
have left. We realized that the lack of conflict had given
Alex an opportunity to think. With no escalation, there
was no stress. With no stress, he could think rather than
just emote.

We have since tried this approach a number of times,
and it has mostly brought forth good fruit. It alleviates
stress in Ariel and me. It avoids conflict. It gives Alex an
opportunity to think through his actions and attitudes. It
also allows us to discuss the situation and the condition of
his heart rationally. This approach isn't *always* effective,
but at this point in his life it is certainly *more* effective.
When it has not brought forth the fruit of repentance, it
has at least left the door open for calm conversation.

If realizing that we needed to think like Alex in order
to understand him was one major breakthrough for us as
adoptive parents, this was a second. To be sure, even today
it feels like we are compromising at times, and I know

some parents would criticize this approach. But here is the bottom line: we now have an approach to correcting Alex that produces more God-glorifying results than we used to get using the heavy hand and words of correction and rebuke.[32]

Alex still needs to learn to receive correction; the Proverbs teach us that anyone who refuses correction is a fool. And we still don't completely understand why Alex behaves this way; we have talked with him, and it seems to be a visceral reaction that goes beyond our understanding. But we do find a marked difference in the results when we avoid escalating the situation and give him some time. This frequently gives us opportunity to speak correctively to him shortly after the conflict has been avoided.

Perhaps something in this chapter has revealed your own sin in dealing with your child. I encourage you to be specific about it and take it to the cross in confession and repentance. But please do not stop there. Go and tell your child what God has shown you, and ask for his or her forgiveness. Take up the passages of Scripture that deal with how you have provoked your child. Pray in those texts and work at defusing conflict. How this looks will vary with the child's age and personality. Talk it over with your spouse. Think about what will work in your family. Think about how you sound when you speak to your child. Think about your tone and your words. Keep the biblical texts in view (Proverbs 15:1, Psalm 141:3, Ephesians 4:29, James 1:19) and ask for the grace to speak words of grace and life. Ask for the grace to be gentle.[33]

Nine
WHEN WE DON'T KNOW WHAT TO DO

In August of 2009, I wrote the following in my journal.

My heart is so conflicted, so heavy, so angry, so confused, so broken, so filled with longing, so filled with despair. I want to cry out to God. I don't want to pray. I want to weep. I don't want to weep. I want to hug Alex. I never want to see him again.

Alex has always been difficult. The difficulties have escalated and seem to have reached a head since he started high school. He is angry. He is disrespectful. He is disobedient. Alex appears to bait Ariel and me. He is constantly provoking us by ignoring us, disrespecting us, or disobeying us—especially his mother. He then turns everything around, acting scared and as if it is all our fault. His actions scream, "I hate you."

His sarcastic comments last night pierced my heart,

"You're a good pastor. People should see you at home. Everybody thinks you are a perfect pastor, but they should see you at home." Later he said, "Why did you even adopt me?" He is more brazen than ever before.

I am afraid that one of these days he may lose it with his mother, sister, or brother. I am afraid that one of these days I will lose it.

I do not know what to do.

What do we do when we feel like things are getting out of control? What do we do when we feel helpless?

This feeling came to a head one Saturday afternoon. We were having a serious conversation with Zach, and I was angry. Alex was disrespectfully lobbing his own opinions into the thick air. He seemed to be the only person who couldn't feel how thick the air was. I politely told Alex he needed to leave the room because he wasn't helping. I said, "I will call you when I am ready to talk to you about what happened."

"No. I am not leaving." His tone was defiant and yet casual. I was shocked. My blood pressure immediately shot up. Gritting my teeth, I said, "You most certainly are going to leave. Now get up and go."

"No Dad, I am not leaving Zach."

Zach tried to make peace. "Alex, it's okay. Just obey Dad."

"No, I am not leaving."

"Yes you are," I said. As I approached him, he moved to *my* recliner.

"What are you going to do? Make me?"

A nuclear bomb of anger went off in my heart. Ariel knew it. She pleaded with me not to lose my temper and then pleaded with Alex to just go to his room. Then he told *her* no.

I lost it. He got up and moved toward me, but I stood my ground. Since Alex outweighed me by at least thirty-five pounds and was about three inches taller, there was not a lot I could do. To my shame, I seriously contemplated punching him in the face. I was so angry. I was so weary of his disrespect toward his mother and me. I was ready and he was ready and things were escalating rapidly. I knew something bad was going to happen. We bumped chests and I felt a surge of rage. Then I told Ariel, "Call 911."

"Are you sure?" I could see the pain and uncertainty on her face.

"Yes. I am tired of this. What other recourse do I have?"

Alex raged, "Oh, you are going to call the cops on your own son? I hate you!"

Then I said it. "That's okay, because I hate you too. I can't stand you. If you won't obey me, I can't physically make you, so we are calling the cops."

At that point it all seemed surreal. This was as bad as it had ever been. Ashley came out of her room, confused as to what was going on. Ariel was crying and dialing 911. Ashley and Zach were begging her not to call. Zach was in tears. It breaks my heart to think of that awful Saturday. The memory of Zach's tears still brings tears to my eyes.

"This is not what our family is about. We aren't like this," Zach pleaded.

"You are right, Zach. This is not what our family is like. This is not what we are about. We are about trying to honor God, we are about respect and love. But your brother has disrupted that, so our family is about something else today!"

Then Ashley blurted out, "Mom is on the phone with 911. Dad, do something." The reality of what was happening began to sink in. Alex sat down on the couch and started to cry. Zach sat back down with a devastated look on his face.

"No, there hasn't been any…Here is my husband." She handed the phone to me.

"Mr. Borgman, has there been violence? Is anyone hurt?"

"No. I think things have calmed down now. I think we will be all right."

"We still need to send an officer out so that he can verify that."

"That's fine. Thank you."

I looked around at my stunned family and said, "An officer is on his way."

We sat there in silence, waiting. The thought came to me, "What will our neighbors think?" That thought was soon followed up with, "It doesn't matter what our neighbors think. This was escalating out of control. My family is suffering under this weight. Dear God, please use this for good."

The officers showed up. I explained everything. I told them to ask the boys whatever they wanted. The boys both confirmed my report. Then the lead officer, who must have been a dad, started asking questions. The boys were exceedingly polite. The officer was appropriately forceful, reinforcing that household rules are the law when you live under your parents' roof.

He then looked at Alex and said, "How old are you? Twenty-one, twenty-two?" Alex softly replied, "I am sixteen."

The officer was in shock. It added a new dimension to his pep talk.

"Sixteen? You are a big guy for sixteen. You are much bigger than your dad."

What a day. After the officers left, we were all in tears. There was an unusual silence in our home, broken only by sobs. I don't know how long it lasted, but it seemed like a month. We hugged. We really hugged. We each took turns holding each other tightly. We asked each other for forgiveness. We all expressed our love for one another. Then we prayed. I had not cried that hard while praying in a long time. I was ashamed. I was relieved. I felt a love for my children and my wife. It was a big tossed salad of emotion.

This is just one story, and for some adoptive families it may seem extreme. Maybe nothing like this has ever happened in your family. You might even be shocked that I just described a pastor's family. For others though, this story was mild by comparison. If that's your family, you probably know the pain of physical altercations, numerous visits by the police, and an extensive list of traumas. What I want to share with you next, I share as a fellow sinner and a fellow struggler. I share not as a preacher who has mastered these principles, but as a dad who knows he has failed more times than he has succeeded—and yet is confident that somehow God's grace will be sufficient.

Grace through Others

When things seem out of control, we need to get help. God has ordained two institutions to help families: the church and the state.

A godly, realistic couple. When we need help, we must realize that God has provided us with the body of Christ—other believers in Jesus who can minister to us. As a general rule, then, the first place to seek help is from other believers, either inside or outside of your own local church. Find a godly couple—people who know you and who are spiritually mature and realistic. If they also have adopted, that's great, but it is not a prerequisite. Many couples may be willing to offer advice, but be careful whom you chose. *Godliness* comes from a close walk with God and a deep knowledge of his Word. *Realism* comes from knowing the human heart, the depth of human sin, the frequent messiness of family relationships, and the power of God's grace.

I have heard many stories from discouraged adoptive parents who have received all kinds of advice and criticism that was completely lacking sympathy and understanding. It's not difficult to find self-appointed experts offering a broad range of input that features easy answers from a black-and-white perspective. Some people seem to think that, whatever your challenge, it's probably a lot like a lawnmower that won't start: a quick diagnosis and a little tinkering are probably all you need to get everything humming again, so what's the big deal?

It's true that when you as an adoptive parent have been doing something wrong, you need godly, constructive counsel and maybe even some painful correction. But you also need to know that your counselors genuinely sympathize with your struggles. You need to know that what you have to say will be heard with patience, and that truth will be spoken in love.

For us, Dave and Diane Gamble have been that voice of godly realism. We know we are safe with them. They understand our weaknesses and flaws, and they don't believe Alex is perfect. Dave's experience as a judge and their collective wisdom from running the City of Refuge give them a refreshing realism. They can correct us or encourage us, and we gladly receive their counsel because we know they love us and understand our situation. When we feel like things are out of control, we go to Dave and Diane. They faithfully help us and point us to the Lord.

Church elders. A second resource we can often forget about as adoptive Christian parents is our local-church eldership. Although we do not today live under the old covenant (which, among other things, endorsed capital punishment and merged civil and ecclesiastical authority into the same set of offices), Mosaic law gave harried parents wise instruction: if a disobedient child is out of control, consult your spiritual elders (Deuteronomy 21:18–20). If you belong to a Bible-believing church that has godly leadership, there may come a time when you need their help and counsel, and your child may need their admonition. They may also see things that you don't see. If the child is a professing Christian and church member, church discipline may even be in order.

The state. God has also ordained the state. In Romans 13:1–4, Paul tells us that God appointed the governing authorities as God's servants for our good. Although the state can overstep its authority—sometimes with disastrous results—we should carefully use the authority of the state when needed.[34] This is what I did when I told Ariel to call 911. Though my heart was not right in that moment we did the right thing, I believe, to lean on the authority of the state for help.[35]

On other occasions, we have met with a juvenile probation officer Dave introduced us to.[36] Although not a Christian, this officer has much common grace and wisdom. Because his work has given him a rare and valuable perspective, he was able to talk frankly to Alex and even offer us specific advice that church members could not. God used this man to help us.

Asking for help requires humility. It is not easy to admit we don't know what to do or don't have answers. It is not easy to acknowledge our failures and confess sins. It is hard to share the problems that live within the four walls of our own homes. We need to remember that when we are reluctant to acknowledge our need for help or let people see our failures, we are operating on the basis of pride. Pride drives us to keep up a nice front, present a nice family, and play the part. Yet "God opposes the proud, but gives grace to the humble" (James 4:6, 1 Peter 5:5).

Ten

WHEN WE DON'T WANT TO DO WHAT WE SHOULD

The story was unthinkable. An adoptive mother in Tennessee put her 7-year-old adopted son on a plane and sent him back to Russia. The picture of a dazed-looking little boy underscored how horrific the act was. The grandmother claimed the boy was violent and had threatened to burn the house down. The boy claimed the mother pulled his hair and the grandmother yelled at him.[37]

My heart breaks for this child. And although I condemn the mother's actions as unconscionable, she obviously was not equipped to handle a little boy who may have been traumatized during his time in a Russian orphanage. If she was willing to send him back, maybe she was unprepared for the depth of his need. If she felt hopeless, my heart goes out to her, because I've been there.

But then I ask, "Who *is* adequate for these things?"

Adoption is a glorious calling. But when the unexpected challenges come, where do we go? What do we do? How do we avoid feeling hopeless?

In this final chapter I would like to encourage you, adoptive parent, by reminding you of some important truths that can help you. There may be times when we don't feel like caring or loving or serving or sacrificing. We may feel like we are at the end of our rope emotionally. How do we press ahead as parents? How do we rekindle enough hope to put one foot in front of the other? How do we resist falling into the snare of the enemy?

The Sovereignty of God

When Alex was little we went on vacation to the Oregon coast. During the drive we listened several times to a Waylon Jennings CD that included the song, "Nothing Catches Jesus by Surprise." Later in the hotel Alex turned to me out of the blue and said, "Daddy, nothing catches Jesus by surprise because he knows everything. Right?"

I told Alex he was right, that God knows everything and plans everything. Then, in a wonderfully memorable moment, I talked to my son about our sovereign God.

Our hearts must be rooted in the truth of God's sovereignty. We must know that "Our God is in the heavens; he does all that he pleases" (Psalm 115:3). We need to embrace from the heart that God really is working out "all things according to the counsel of his will" (Ephesians 1:11). We must marinate in the truth that "For from him and through him and to him are all things. To him be the glory forever" (Romans 11:36). There are no accidents in

God's universe. There is no such thing as fortune or fate. Nothing takes God by surprise. There is only the will of God. This is not always easy for our finite minds to fathom, but it is a bedrock truth of Scripture that believers have always held dear.

This means that every adoptive parent is each in their own situation and circumstances by the wise, loving decision of a gracious God. That adopted child is yours by a sovereign act of the Lord of heaven and earth, not by chance. During the tough times, we need to remember that God does have a plan for our adopted children—and for us. He never makes a mistake. I have preached to myself that Alex is ours by God's sovereign purpose and plan. Ariel and I have reminded each other many times that Alex is our son and we are his parents by God's will. God's ways and plans are perfect—in our situation and in yours.

Our Merciful and Faithful High Priest

The knowledge of God's sovereignty is a powerful tonic in our times of weak and wavering faith. But it's not enough by itself. We also need to be deeply connected to Jesus as our merciful and faithful High Priest. The writer to the Hebrews says,

> Therefore he had to be made like his brothers in every respect, so that he might become a merciful and faithful high priest in the service of God, to make propitiation for the sins of the people. For because he

himself has suffered when tempted, he is able to help those who are being tempted (Hebrews 2:17–18).

And later,

For we do not have a high priest who is unable to sympathize with our weaknesses, but one who in every respect has been tempted as we are, yet without sin. Let us then with confidence draw near to the throne of grace, that we may receive mercy and find grace to help in time of need (Hebrews 4:15–16).

We need to understand at a deep heart level that Jesus knows and sympathizes with our weaknesses. He is also merciful. The Puritan John Owen said that Jesus is "one that lays all the miseries of his people to heart, so caring for them, to relieve them."[38] Jesus the Son of God is merciful to you in your weakness as a parent. But he is also faithful. He is utterly reliable. He prays for you (Hebrews 7:25) and is always there for you. He also is ready to pour out grace when we need it. There is no shortage of mercy and help from the throne of grace.

Parents, run to our Great High Priest with your sins and find peace and power in him. Take your sins of impatience, despondency, anger, and hard-heartedness to the cross. Find fresh forgiveness through the Son. C.H. Spurgeon, the prince of preachers, said,

Great thoughts of your sin alone will drive you to despair; but great thoughts of Christ will pilot you into the haven of peace. "My sins are many, but oh! it is nothing to Jesus to take them all away. The weight of my guilt presses me down as a giant's foot would crush a worm, but it is no more than a grain of dust to him, because he has already borne its curse in his own body on the tree."[39]

If my own heart is to be renewed to keep on loving and serving, then it must be refreshed through knowing Jesus' mercy and love to me. As I soak in the love and mercy of Jesus towards me, I am invigorated in my heart to show love and mercy in return. As I get fresh supplies of grace at the throne of grace, I am equipped to extend grace. The only way I can be a conduit of grace and mercy to a difficult child is if I am receiving grace and mercy on a daily basis.

The Gospel of Adoption

Finally, the gospel of adoption must be preached to ourselves over and over again. God brought me in by his grace. He will not stop loving me or kick me out of his family. His love for me is secure (Romans 8:38–39). Although he may discipline me, I never stop being his child (John 10:27–29). He is committed to seeing this work through to its completion (Philippians 1:6). Such truth can indeed empower us to turn around and show the same grace to our child.

We can pray, "Father, since you never stop loving me, help me to keep loving him. Give me your faithful determination to gracefully see this through to completion. Give me grace every step of the way so I may finish the work."

Final Reflections

Alex is 18 now. He still lives at home and we still have problems. Ariel and I continue to sin and make mistakes. So does Alex. So we continue to ask forgiveness from God and one another, and continue to grant it freely whenever needed—or at least we try. Through it all, the gospel is immeasurably precious to us.

But neither Ariel nor I can imagine what life would have been like without Alex in our home. We shudder to think where he would be if he weren't our son. He said to me the other day, "Dad, I am glad you adopted me, otherwise I probably wouldn't have become a redneck. I would probably be in jail." Well, I wish he had said "Christian" instead of "redneck," but I am glad that he is glad to be in our family.

When Alex turned 18, Ariel and I felt we had reached a milestone. By God's grace we brought him to legal adulthood. There is still more work to do, and still more lessons to learn, but God is faithful. In the midst of the grit of adoption, there is an abundance of grace. The challenges are great, but grace is greater. Christ is enough.

A Word to Prospective Adoptive Parents

I hope you rescue and minister to a child in need. I hope you march into enemy territory and bring a child out of darkness. But if you are thinking about adoption, please go in with your eyes wide open, with a view to ministry, remembering that you are trekking into enemy territory and are going to do something that is, in a way, God-like.

There's only one way to do that—you will need grace. You may not need as much grit as we've needed, but you will still need grace. You may need more grit—a lot more. Perhaps your story will make ours look like a fairy tale. Still, you will need grace.

Be flexible. Be transparent. Rely on the body of Christ. Take up the full armor of God. You will need it, for parenting is a hard calling under the most ideal circumstances. I hope that this book has helped prepare you for what may be some difficult times.

A Word to Adoptive Parents

If you have already adopted and they are yours, I trust there have been truths in this book that have helped you. Perhaps your story has not had nearly the bumps that ours has had. Perhaps you are much better parents than we are, far more wise and patient. Perhaps your struggles have run much deeper than ours. In any event, I pray that the Holy Spirit has ministered to you through these pages. I hope that the gospel and the truths of God's Word have refreshed you.

Finally, let us remember that the gospel not only motivates us to adopt, the gospel sustains us after they are ours.

Appendix
PARENTING IN GENTLENESS

The opposite of escalation and provocation is meekness or gentleness. As I have studied the relevant words used in Scripture, I have concluded that meekness is a gentle, courteous humility that is considerate of the condition and circumstances of others. It is the opposite of harshness. We desperately need meekness or gentleness when we interact with our children. Consider these biblical truths.

Gentleness is consistent with the Spirit of Christ. Jesus said, "I am gentle and lowly in heart" (Matthew 11:29). "I, Paul, myself entreat you, by the meekness and gentleness of Christ"(2 Corinthians 10:1)

Gentleness is contrary to a disciplinarian spirit. "What do you wish? Shall I come to you with a rod, or with love in a spirit of gentleness (meekness)?" (1 Corinthians 4:21).

Gentleness is a fruit of the Spirit. "But the fruit of the Spirit is love, joy, peace, patience, kindness, goodness, faithfulness, gentleness, self-control; against such things there is no law" (Galatians 5:22–23).

Gentleness is a Christian virtue that we must wear and exercise towards everyone. "Walk in a manner worthy of the calling to which you have been called, with all humility and gentleness, with patience bearing with one another in love" (Ephesians 4:1–2). "Put on then, as God's chosen ones, holy and beloved, compassionate hearts, kindness, humility, meekness, and patience" (Colossians 3:12). "Show perfect courtesy toward all people" (Titus 3:2).

Meekness is needed when disciplining and correcting. "Brothers, if anyone is caught in any transgression, you who are spiritual should restore him in a spirit of gentleness" (Galatians 6:1). "And the Lord's servant must not be quarrelsome but kind to everyone…correcting his opponents with gentleness" (2 Timothy 2:24–25).

Meekness is an essential aspect of Christian wisdom. "Who is wise and understanding among you? By his good conduct let him show his works in the meekness of wisdom" (James 3:13).

A Christian parent should manifest the Spirit of Christ, bear the fruit of the Spirit, and exercise wisdom from above. It should be clear from these verses that meekness/gentleness is an indispensable trait of the Christian parent. Matthew Henry notes, "Superiors are commonly very apt to chide, and that is for want (lack) of meekness."[40] He observes that when people have authority over children, they can mistakenly believe their harshness is necessary.

The undue and intemperate passion of superiors goes under the umbrage and excuse of necessary strictness, and the maintaining of authority, and the education and control of children... But surely every little failure need not be censured…Is this the best badge of your authority you have to put on?[41]

When children feel as if they are always in trouble, or always on the verge of getting in trouble, when they feel little mercy and virtually no consideration for their childishness, their hearts are hardened and they become exasperated (Ephesians 6:4, Colossians 3:21). Charles Bridges reminds us that discipline is "medicine, not food."[42]

Children need someone who will exercise meekness with them, even when they are being corrected or disciplined. They need someone who understands that many of their offenses come, not necessarily because of rebellion, but because of childish weakness. They need to know they are loved, and they need this demonstrated not merely by words, but by real gentleness and forbearance.

This brings up the last point regarding meekness. A meek heart does not find a personal insult in every act of disobedience. A meek heart responds to a child's disobedience with patience, a willingness to hear, a willingness to be wrong, and a desire to help the child see their disobedience in light of Christ's cross and the forgiveness of God. Meekness *will* correct and discipline, but it will be permeated with gentleness and love. Christ-like meekness will make a home a safe place for children to grow and see the gospel in action.

Author

Brian Borgman is the author of several books, a contributor to the *Women's ESV Devotional Bible*, and founding pastor of Grace Community Church, Minden, NV (1993-present). He earned a B.A. in Biblical Studies from Biola University (La Mirada, CA), a Master of Divinity from Western Conservative Baptist Seminary (Portland, OR) and a Doctor of Ministry from Westminster Seminary (Escondido, CA). Brian and his wife, Ariel, have been married since 1987 and have three children and one grandchild.

Acknowledgments & Dedication

Although this book is short, it took a long time to write. In some ways it took three years, in other ways it took seventeen. Those years have been filled with people who have helped us in this wonderful journey. There are the people who encouraged us to adopt and the people who supported us through the challenging times. Ariel and I did not always see eye to eye on how to parent, but I thank God for a wife who loves the Lord her God, loves me, and loves Alex. Thank you, Ariel, for being you. You are a gift.

Of course, none of this journey would have existed without Alex, our son. Alex, you are a gift to us and you have taught us so much. We pray that you flourish in Christ and his grace.

Zach, I am so thankful that you and your brother are such good friends. It is a blessing to see you look out for him.

Ashley, God has blessed you with two loyal brothers who are now proud uncles.

I want to thank the wonderful servants of Christ at Cruciform Press. It is obvious to me that you all love what you do and do it for the glory of Christ and the good of the church. May the Lord bless your labors. Bob Bevington, thank you for calling me and expressing interest and support and giving me good advice and encouragement. Kevin Meath, thank you for seeing this through with care. Jennifer Strange, working with an editor can be humbling. You made the book better. Thanks.

Dan Cruver, from Together for Adoption, thank you for your strong encouragement. Your words strengthened my resolve when I was wavering over whether or not it was worth it to write this book. Thank you for the Foreword. Thank you most of all for your untiring work on behalf of orphans. Your work reverberates with God's grace.

To all who have adopted and practiced pure and undefiled religion, may your tribe increase throughout the earth!

This book is dedicated to the loving memory of our very dear friend, Diane Gamble. You will meet Diane in the pages of this book. She went to heaven, unexpectedly, during the production of this book. There are many people alive and thriving today because of Diny's work against abortion and for adoption. Ariel and I are so grateful that she was such a big part of the Borgman family.

> *"Blessed are the dead who die in the Lord from now on!" "Blessed indeed," says the Spirit, "that they may rest from their labors, for their deeds follow them!"*
>
> Revelation 14:13

Endnotes

1. Russell Moore, *Adopted For Life* (Wheaton: Crossway, 2009), 204–205, 214. Again, let me emphasize that I think Moore's book is very good. It is exceptionally well written and inspiring, and it advocates for adoption in a powerful way. I'm also certain these passages were written with the best of intentions, and that many readers receive them as helpful and edifying. In part, I quote this passage because it represents a not-uncommon perspective with respect to adoption difficulties and that this perspective, for some adoptive parents, is troubling and unhelpful through no fault of their own.

2. Paul DavidTripp, *Helping Your Adopted Child* (Greensboro, NC: New Growth Press, 2008), 4, 6.

3. Koinonia Ministries has expanded over the years to cover other vital areas. Visit them at www.kfh.org.

4. Maggie Jones, "God CalledThem to Adopt. And Adopt. And Adopt." *New York Times* (November 14, 2013), http://www.nytimes.com/2013/11/17/magazine/god-called-them-to-adopt-and-adopt-and-adopt.html.

5. Since that time, the laws in Nevada have changed so that the process is not so long and drawn out when there is no effort on the parents' part.

6. Emily Belz, "Not *Annie the Musical*," World Magazine (November 30, 2013): 47, http://www.worldmag.com/2013/11/not_annie_the_musical.

7. When I originally preached on adoption around 2002, there was not much available on the doctrine of adoption (John Murray, J. I. Packer and J. L Girardeau had excellent theological treatments and Robert Peterson's *Adopted By God* had just been released), so I am grateful for the number of good books available now. They include *Reclaiming Adoption: Missional Living through the Rediscovery of Abba Father* (Dan Cruver, ed., Cruciform Press, 2011), *Heirs with Christ: The Puritans on Adoption* (Joel Beeke, ed., Reformation Heritage Books, 2008), *Adopted into God's Family: Exploring a Pauline Metaphor* (Trevor J. Burke, IVP Academic, 2006), and *A Hope Deferred: Adoption and the Fatherhood of God* (J. Stephen Yuille, Shepherd Press, 2013).

8. J. I. Packer, *Knowing God* (Downers Grove, IL: InterVarsity Press, 1993), 202.

9. John R. W. Stott, *The Message of Galatians* (Leicester, England: Inter-Varsity, 1968), 107.

10. Packer, 207.

11. I am not minimizing the good work done by many wonderful Christian orphanages. I am speaking of institutions, foreign or domestic, where children are not cared for by followers of Christ.

12. Julie Smith Lowe, "Counseling the Adopted Child," *The Journal of Biblical Counseling* (Winter 2007): 42. I recommend Lowe's article (reprinted at http://www.togetherforadoption. org/wp-content/media/counseling-the-adopted-child.pdf) for a loving and realistic discussion of the challenges that adoptive families might face, whether their child has been in their family from birth or has encountered very difficult experiences.

13. Karyn Purvis, David Cross, and Wendy Lyons Sunshine, *The Connected Child* (New York: McGraw Hill, 2007), 23–24.

14. Sherrie Eldridge, *Twenty Things Adopted Kids Wish Their Adoptive Parents Knew* (New York: Delta, 1999), 85–95.

15. See Brian Borgman and Rob Ventura, *Spiritual Warfare: A Biblical and Balanced Perspective* (Grand Rapids: Reformation Heritage Books, 2014).

16. I heartily recommend Joshua Mack's blog posts on adoption as war (see the five-part series as well as other adoption-related posts at http://joshnmarda.wordpress.com/category/adoption/) and his message, "Adoption Is War" given at the Together for Adoption South Africa Conference 2014 (http://www. adoptionconference.co.za/index.php?option=com_content&vie w=article&id=182&Itemid=218).

17. Paul Tripp, *Age of Opportunity* (Phillipsburg, NJ: Presbyterian and Reformed, 2001), 31.

18. For more on the relationship between desires and demands, see Paul David Tripp, *Instruments in the Redeemer's Hands* (Phillipsburg, NJ: P&R, 2002), 86.

19. Eldridge, 16.

20. For more gospel-centered counsel on the subject of romanticizing adoption, I recommend three posts published by the Together for Adoption blog: T4A director Dan Cruver wrote the first two in the series (http://www.togetherforadoption. org/?p=18447 and http://www.togetherforadoption. org/?p=18520), and Angela Prince, PhD, wrote the third (and http://www.togetherforadoption.org/?p=18606).

21. Jay Adams, *Christian Living in the Home* (Phillipsburg, NJ: P&R, 1972), 10.

22. See William Farley's helpful distinction between offensive and defensive parenting in the first chapter of *Gospel-Powered*

Parenting (Philipsburg, NJ: P&R, 2009).

23. Family reputation is very important, but can never be our main concern.

24. John Calvin, *Institutes* 1.11.8.

25. Tripp, *Helping Your Adopted Child*, 7, emphasis added.

26. Rosaria Champagne Butterfield, *The Secret Thoughts of an Unlikely Convert* (Pittsburgh: Crown and Covenant, 2012), 126.

27. Eldridge, 7–8.

28. Paul David Tripp, *Instruments in the Redeemer's Hands* (Phillipsburg, NJ: Presbyterian and Reformed, 2002), 41. (Emphasis in original)

29. Eldridge, 31, 32.

30. Lou Priolo, *The Heart of Anger* (Amityville, NY: Calvary, 1997), 30–51.

31. Tripp, *Helping Your Adopted Child*, 7.

32. Whether this modified approach would have worked as well when Alex was significantly younger, I can't say.

33. See the Appendix

34. George Scipione's address from the Institute of Biblical Counseling and Discipleship offers a helpful overview of the use of the church and state. http://www.ibcd.org/resources/messages/how-to-handle-rebellious-dangerous-teens/

35. To use the authority of the state carefully parents must investigate local resources before trouble comes. Talking to local law enforcement officers or lawyers in your church may be a good start. As noted in the next paragraph, a juvenile probation officer may be a good choice, especially if there has been no offense. Often local JPOs are willing to help on an informal basis.

36. If possible, ask those you may know who are in law enforcement or the legal profession for a recommendation.

37. http://abcnews.go.com/WN/anger-mom-adopted-boy-back-russia/story?id=10331728

38. John Owen, *An Exposition of the Epistle to the Hebrews, with Preliminary Exercitations* (London: Thomas Tegg, 1840), 2:417.

39. Charles Spurgeon, "March 27 Evening," *Morning and Evening* (Peabody, MA: Hendrickson, 1995), 175.

40. Matthew Henry, *The Quest for Meekness and Quietness of Spirit* (Eugene, OR: Wipf and Stock, 2007), 83. I cannot recommend this little book highly enough!

41. Henry, 84.

42. Charles Bridges, *An Exposition of the Book of Proverbs* (New York: Robert Carter, 1847), 364.

Wrestling with an Angel
A Story of Love, Disability
and the Lessons of Grace

by Greg Lucas

**The riveting, inspiring true story
that readers have called
"a touchstone book of my life,"
and "alternately hilarious and
heartbreaking," a book that
"turns the diamond of grace in
such a way that you see facets
you never really noticed before."**

*92 pages
Learn more at bit.ly/CPWrestle*

"C.S. Lewis wrote that he paradoxically loved *The Lord of the Rings*
because it 'broke his heart'—and Greg Lucas' writing does the same
for me."
Justin Taylor, Managing Editor, ESV Study Bible

"Witty... stunning... striking... humorous and heartfelt. *Wrestling with an
Angel* provides a fresh, honest look at one father's struggle to embrace
God in the midst of his son's disability. Can sheer laughter and weep-
ing gracefully coexist in a world of so much affliction? Greg knows all
about it. I highly recommend this wonderfully personal book!"
Joni Eareckson Tada, Joni and Friends International

"You will laugh; you will cry. You will feel sick; you will feel inspired.
You will be repulsed by the ugliness of sin; you will be overwhelmed
by the love of God. Greg Lucas takes us on an unforgettable ride as he
extracts the most beautiful insights into grace from the most painful
experiences of life."
David P. Murray, Puritan Reformed Theological Seminary

"Greg Lucas is a captivating storyteller. When he writes about life with
Jake, I recognize God's grace and loving persistence in my life. I want
more!"
Noël Piper, author, and wife of pastor and author John Piper

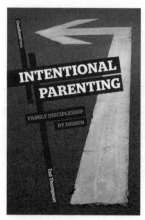

Intentional Parenting
Family Discipleship by Design

by Tad Thompson

**The Big Picture and a Simple Plan —
That's What You Need to Do Family
Discipleship Well**

*This book will allow you to take all the
sermons, teachings, and exhortations
you have received on the topic of
family discipleship, make sense of it,
and put it to use.*

102 pp. Learn more at bit.ly/IParent

"As parents, we know God has given us the responsibility to train our
children in his ways. But many parents don't know where or how to
start. Tad has done us all a favor by identifying seven key categories
of biblical teaching we can utilize in teaching our children godly
truth and principles. This easy-to-follow plan will help any parent
put the truth of God's Word into their children's hearts."

> **Kevin Ezell, President, North American Mission Board,
> Southern Baptist Convention; father of six**

"Here is a practical page-turner that encourages fathers to engage the
hearts of their families with truth and grace. In an age when truth is
either ignored or despised, it is refreshing to see a book written for
ordinary fathers who want their families to be sanctified by the truth.
Thompson writes with a grace which reminds us that parenting
flows from the sweet mercies of Christ."

> **Joel Beeke, President, Puritan Reformed Theological
> Seminary**

"Need an introductory text to the topic of discipling children? Here is
a clear, simple book on family discipleship, centered on the gospel
rather than human successes or external behaviors."

> **James M. Hamilton, Associate Professor of Biblical
> Theology, The Southern Baptist Theological Seminary**

Torn to Heal
God's Good Purpose in Suffering
by Mike Leake

**Recieve comfort for today.
Be prepared to for tomorrow.**

*87 pages
Learn more at bit.ly/TORN2H*

"The most concise, readable, and helpful theology of suffering I've come across. The content, length, and tone is just perfect for those who are in the furnace of affliction screaming 'Why?'"
Dr. David Murray, Puritan Reformed Theological Seminary

"Mike Leake has taken the ugliness of suffering, turned it over in his capable hands, and shown God's goodness and faithfulness in the midst. More than simple encouragement, it is a handbook of scriptural truths about Who God is and how He sustains."
Lore Ferguson writes for Gospel Coalition, CBMW, and more

"A gospel-driven path between dualism that acts as if God has lost control of his world and fatalism/stoicism that tries to bury pain beneath emotionless acceptance of whatever happens. The result is a brief but potent primer on the purpose of suffering."
Timothy Paul Jones, Southern Baptist Theological Seminary

"Explores God's redemptive purposes in human suffering in a concise, biblical and authentic way. Mike shuns cliches and platitudes to help the reader put life's hardships into divine perspective and to endure in Christ's strength. It is a must-read for Christians in distress."
Dave Miller, Second Vice-President, Southern Baptist Convention

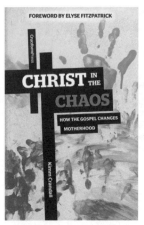

Christ in the Chaos
How the Gospel Changes Motherhood

by Kimm Crandall

MOMS: Stop comparing yourself to others. Stop striving to meet false expectations. Stop thinking your performance dictates your worth.

Look to the gospel for rest, joy, sufficiency, identity, and motivation.

113 pp, Learn more at bit.ly/Christ-in

"Although Kimm Crandall's message would revive any soul longing for the breath of the gospel of grace, I am especially eager to recommend this book to that heart who strives to know God and to make him known to the little ones who call her 'Momma.' Kimm is a candid and gracious fellow sojourner, faithfully pointing to God's immeasurable steadfast love and grace in the midst of our mess."

Lauren Chandler, wife of Matt Chandler (pastor of The Village Church), mother of three, writer, singer, and speaker

"What an amazingly wild and wise, disruptive and delighting, freeing and focusing book. Kimm's book is for every parent willing to take the stewardship of children and the riches of the gospel seriously. This is one of the most helpful and encouraging books on parenting I've read in the past twenty years. This will be a book you will want to give to parents, to-be parents, and grandparents."

Scotty Smith, author; Founding Pastor, Christ Community Church

"Kimm Crandall has discovered that chaos can be the perfect context in which to experience God's liberating grace. She is a wise, practical, gospel-drenched guide for anyone navigating through the wearisome terrain of parenting."

Tullian Tchividjian, author; Pastor, Coral Ridge Presbyterian Church